LAGNIAPPE LEFTOVERS

D1572817

Susanne Duplantis

PELICAN PUBLISHING
New Orleans

Copyright © 2022
By Susanne Duplantis
All rights reserved

The word "Pelican" and the depiction of a pelican are
trademarks of Arcadia Publishing Company Inc. and are
registered in the U.S. Patent and Trademark Office.

Library of Congress Cataloging-in-Publication Data

Names: Duplantis, Susanne, author. | Quaid, Tom, illustrator.
Title: Lagniappe leftovers / Susanne Duplantis ; illustrations by Tom Quaid.
Description: New Orleans : Pelican Publishing, 2022. | Includes index. | Summary: "Food-waste chef and blogger Susanne Duplantis presents here her cookbook that repurposes Southern leftovers to save food and money. These 100 recipes and twenty-five tips are offered with the charm of an old cookbook that has been passed down from generation to generation. If Southern cooking is in your soul, you will delight in these creative ideas for making the best use of your delicious leftovers"— Provided by publisher.
Identifiers: LCCN 2021050937 | ISBN 9781455626540 (paperback) | ISBN 9781455626557 (ebook)
Subjects: LCSH: Cooking (Leftovers) | Cooking, American—Southern style. | LCGFT: Cookbooks.
Classification: LCC TX652 .D866 2022 | DDC 641.5/52—dc23/eng/20211027
LC record available at https://lccn.loc.gov/2021050937

Illustrations by Tom Quaid

Printed in the United States of America

Published by Pelican Publishing
New Orleans, LA
www.pelicanpub.com

For MeMaw

(1920-85)

Contents

Acknowledgments

To my number-one fan, my mom, thank you for your daily support and encouragement. To my husband, who claims to be "just a man living off leftovers," thank you for your love of me and of leftovers and for the hours of dishwashing. To my family and friends, thanks for your love, support, and days of taste testing.

To Lauren, thanks for giving me my start on television. To Lilian, thanks for seeing the value in leftovers. To Celeste, thanks for my blog motivation.

To Dr. Tom Quaid, there are no words to express my deep gratitude for your beautiful gift of illustrations that brought this book to life.

To Pelican Publishing, thanks for making my dream a reality.

INTRODUCTION

My culinary background began on a stepstool in my grandmother's kitchen in Algiers, Louisiana. I called her MeMaw. I was her pot stirrer, flour sifter, potato masher, carrot peeler, egg whisker, and official taste tester. I was her sous chef and that was way before I ever knew what that meant. MeMaw not only taught me the basics of cooking; she taught me the most valuable lesson in the kitchen. From gathering fresh vegetables from her garden to eating the very last morsel of food picked or prepared, she taught me the value of food.

Any food leftover from breakfast found its way into lunch, and any leftovers from dinner were certain to be a part of breakfast the next day. Scraps became ingredients for stocks, seeds were replanted, and no morsel was ever too small not to save.

One of my earliest memories of a cookbook was from first grade. My mom gave me money for our school book sale and I remember excitedly picking out a book with a beautiful bowl of food on the front. When my mom picked me up that afternoon, I was eager to show her my purchase. She was pleased because it would teach me how to set a table, and MeMaw was excited because it would teach me more about cooking. A section in the book titled "How to Be a Good Cook" provided simple advice: eat and enjoy the food you have made, and share it when you can. I still have that cookbook and it has always inspired me to write one of my own. I would have never guessed my cookbook would be about leftovers, but then again, leftovers have always been a part of my life in some way or another.

Some of the greatest Southern dishes originated from leftovers. In the South, we turn what others throw away into delicacies—hushpuppies, boudin, and gumbo all take their essence from leftovers. Whether using leftover cornmeal to make hushpuppies, every bit of a hog to make boudin, or leftover scraps of sausage, seafood, or fowl for gumbo, Southern cooks have learned to create meals using whatever ingredients are readily available. Some Southern traditions, such as red beans and rice Mondays, grew from the habit of finishing leftover pork chops, ham, or a hambone from Sunday's dinner while the laundry was being done.

Everyone in the South has their favorite recipes for these classics. This book takes the last bit of leftovers from those recipes and repurposes them into brand-new tasty offerings while saving on money. These simple home-cooking recipes use the time-saving advantage of leftovers along with easy-to-find ingredients.

Let's begin by thinking outside the box. Yes, think outside the icebox full of leftovers and see "leftovers as start overs" to save time, food, and money.

MAKEOVER MY LEFTOVER

Working in the restaurant industry for more than twenty years, I saw my fair share of food waste. From the kitchen in the back of the house to the customers in the front, refusal to make use of ingredients or take home to-go boxes was a daily reality. My MeMaw's lesson of valuing food always weighed on me. I began to write short suggestions for the leftovers on to-go boxes, and to my delight, more customers began to take them home.

After suffering a stroke, I left the restaurant business but could not forget about the food waste. A chef friend suggested I start a food blog. I did. When I started my blog, Makeover My Leftover, in 2014, my main goal was to help just one family save food and money. Most food waste occurs in the home, so I focused on my own. Did the girl who grew up being taught to value food become a woman who wasted it? Sadly yes.

I kept a close eye on what food was being wasted, and to my surprise it was coming right off the plates of my family. I then realized it was the plate size. We were each loading our dish, but it was more than we could eat. I donated my big, beautiful, deep plates and purchased smaller ones, and to my satisfaction that food stopped going into the trash.

The rest of the food in my trash was "scraps." This set me on the journey of developing recipes for leftover scraps, such as apple or pineapple cores and banana peels. (Want to keep your roast moist? Toss in a banana peel as it cooks!) It also got me started on composting.

I began sharing my discoveries about food waste on my blog, mainly as a record of my own. I had the crazy idea that I could have a food blog that simply offered tips and suggestions without recipes. I didn't want to contribute to food waste by having readers buy all the ingredients for a recipe when they could possibly substitute with items they already had on hand. The number of people who requested a recipe began to grow. I quickly realized my original idea was not completely working, so I started offering recipes along with the tips and suggestions.

Soon after I began Makeover My Leftover, it was featured on a news segment called "Money Mondays." I happily realized that my new purpose and passion could be to help others save food and money. I began to teach food-waste workshops.

Here are a few tips to help save food that I highlight in my workshops:

1. *Be Safe:* The FDA recommends that refrigerators be kept at 40 degrees or below and freezers at 0 degrees or below for food safety. Leftovers should not be left out at room temperature for longer than two hours. A tip I recommend is freezing a container of water and placing a penny on top of the water. If you later find that the penny sank partially or all the way into the water, it's a good indication that the power went out and for how long. Of course, the old adage "when in doubt, throw it out" can be followed.

Filming the TV premiere of "Makeover My Leftover."

2. *Take the Challenge:* Don't think you have much food waste? For one week, keep a separate bag of *all* peelings, scraps, discarded leftovers from home and restaurants, and spoiled food. At the end of the week, you can *see* all your food waste. They say out of sight means out of mind, and they also say seeing is believing. How much money is in that one bag of food trash?

3. *Take Inventories:* Create inventory sheets for your freezer, pantry, and fridge. Take inventory often. This will save you time, money, and energy when planning meals. I keep an inventory sheet on the front of the freezer, so there is no need to open the freezer to see what is available.

4. *Take It with You:* Carry an insulated lunch tote in your car to take home leftovers from restaurants. There will be no excuse not to bring them home or back to the office. Simply ask for a cup of ice with your to-go box. There may be a minimal charge for the ice, but it will be worth it.

5. *Get Chillin':* Make your freezer your BFF, because just about anything can be frozen. Use containers, wraps, and bags appropriate for items being stored in the freezer, and use the smallest possible container to hold the leftovers in order to reduce air. Remember to date and label *everything.* Buy ice-cube trays and then use them to freeze leftover tomato paste, brewed coffee and tea, stock, gravy, sauce, or fresh herbs in olive oil. Place the frozen cubes in containers in the freezer. They'll always be at the ready for cooking.

6. *Prioritize:* Follow the FIFO (First In, First Out) rule when stocking the fridge

with groceries. Place new items behind older ones. Make an Eat First box by setting a box or bowl front and center in your fridge. Then add everything that needs to be eaten first. Think of the things that get hidden in a drawer or lost on the shelf, such as the last slice of cheese or bit of mayo, browning apple slices, etc.

7. *Stock Up:* Make stocks from rotisserie chicken carcasses, hambones, shrimp shells, fish bones, or corncobs. Save onion peelings, celery tops, and other vegetable scraps in a bag in the freezer. When the bag is full, use the contents to make a vegetable stock or add to other stocks.

8. *Keep Growing:* Plant the seeds from fruits and vegetables. Regrow lettuce, celery, green onions, and herbs. Here are instructions to get you started.

- Celery: Place celery bottom in bowl of water. Change water daily. Watch new leaves sprout. Plant in ground after one week.
- Lettuce: Put core in water. Change water daily. Eat new growth, just enough for a BLT. Watch for roots, then plant.
- Green onions: Place roots in water. Watch the roots grow. Change water every few days, or plant in ground. Just like Jack's beanstalk, they will keep growing and growing each time they are cut.
- Herbs: Place stem in glass of water, with any leaves above water. Watch for roots, then plant.

9. *Know It:* I do a whole segment on the "best by" date in my workshops. It can be very confusing and is the reason why 60 percent of food is prematurely thrown away. Do you know what is the only item required by the FDA to have a date label? Infant formula. Didn't guess it? None of my workshop attendees ever do either. In short, "best by" or "best if used by" is a manufacturer's suggestion. It is all about quality not safety. There are some wonderful salvage stores that sell products past these dates. Those stores offer an amazing opportunity to save food and tons of money. The "sell by" date is strictly for the store staff to know how long to keep an item on a shelf. There are usually extra days built into the date.

10. *Love It:* Love the food you bought and love the ones who grew it, made it, packaged it, hauled it, stocked it, and bagged it. This way you appreciate not only all the people who made the food possible but also all the resources used. For instance, tossing away one apple is like pouring 25 gallons of water down a drain. Of course, none of us would ever do that, but have any of us every thrown away an apple? Love the ugly, imperfect fruits and vegetables, too.

11. *Process It:* A mini food processor is one of the greatest food-waste fighters when it comes to repurposing leftovers. I highly recommend buying one if you don't already have one. You will see in this book just how handy this gadget can be.

12. *Supply It:* To transform leftovers more easily, it helps to have some staple supplies on hand beyond just flour, sugar, etc. I like to have items that have multiple uses. For instance, pita bread and tortillas can be used for sandwiches and also to make chips. Here is my go-to supply list. Use it as a guide and adjust it to your family's likes and dislikes.

Pantry List:
- **Assorted rices**—flavored microwave ones are good in a pinch, but watch the sodium levels
- **Stocks or broths**—chicken, beef, and vegetable, for soups and sauces
- **Assorted pastas**—for hot meals, cold pasta salads, and sides
- **Canned tomatoes/tomato sauce/baked beans**—for soups, sauces, and pasta
- **Canned corn**—for soups and casseroles
- **Dried and canned beans**—for beans and rice, soups, burritos, and bean burgers
- **Salmon and/or tuna pouches**—add to hot or cold pasta, mashed potatoes, omelettes, or fritters
- **Grits/polenta**—for breakfast and as base for serving tomatoes, vegetables, or leftovers
- **Instant mashed potatoes**—use in soups, as base for serving leftovers, as base/topping of a savory pie, or as coating for fish
- **Cornbread mix**—for casseroles such as tamale pie, sides, muffins, fritters, or pancakes
- **Organic canned chicken**
- **Nuts**—as a snack but also to use as coating for fish or chicken
- **Crackers**—crush and use like breadcrumbs
- **Popcorn**
- **Coconut milk**—for curry and ice cream
- **Peanut butter**
- **Honey**—never goes bad!

Freezer List:
- **Vegetables**
- **Seasonings**—including chopped onions, bell peppers, celery, or combination
- **Fruit**—including lemons and limes
- **Bread and rolls**
- **IQF (Individually Quick Frozen) shrimp**
- **Burgers or veggie burgers**
- **Pork chops, chicken, and/or fish**
- **Sausage**

Refrigerator List:
(Note: I only stock with items that can be frozen)
- **Cheese**
- **Tortillas and/or pita bread**—for quesadillas, burritos, wraps, sandwiches, and chips
- **Hummus**

- Olives
- Carrots
- Eggs*
- Cured meats
- **Wonton wrappers**—for ravioli, pot stickers, fried wontons, and wonton soup
- **Roll-out pizza dough**—for calzones, pizza, and pinwheels
- Butter

*Before freezing eggs in a container, crack them open and whisk together. Whites and yolks can be kept separate by freezing in a silicone ice-cube tray before adding to a container. If preferred, single eggs can be whisked, frozen in a silicone muffin tin, then transferred to an airtight container. Eggs can last up to a year in the freezer and are easily thawed in the refrigerator overnight.

Now that you are set and ready, it's time to put on your "To Cook Is to Create" thinking cap and release your inner culinary artist. Most recipes in this book have a "To Cook Is to Create" section, offering suggestions for using what you already have on hand to create a new leftover favorite for your family.

Big Fun on the Bayou

Jambalaya, Etouffée, Gumbo

JAMBALAYA

Jambalaya is the Southern version of paella, thanks to the early Spanish settlers in Louisiana. Traditional paella ingredients such as saffron could not be found, so the cooks used the abundance of tomatoes instead. It sounds like an early "To Cook Is to Create" culinary move. Ironically, whether or not to add tomatoes to jambalaya has become a cause for debate around the kettle today.

The fact that there are jambalaya kettles, or cauldrons, and jambalaya paddles proves there is no such thing as a small jambalaya pot. Big, black, steaming cauldrons of jambalaya can be seen at fundraisers, festivals, and football games. Football tailgating can be a delightful sensory experience. In fact, one can just follow one's nose around, finding the black bubbling pots laden with sausage, seafood, chicken, vegetables, or the weekend's hunting trophy. Depending on the season, anything goes into the kettle, from fresh seasonings and homegrown vegetables to the catch or kill of the day. There definitely is room for improvisation. Every year, I attend a jambalaya cooking party where each guest brings a "gift" for the pot.

There are two things you can always count on with jambalaya: no two cooks ever prepare it the same way, and there are always leftovers. Having leftover jambalaya is like having extra time on your hands, for it is truly a recipe timesaver.

Another advantage of leftover jambalaya is it makes a quick and easy stuffing. No matter the combination of meats, seafood, or poultry in the jambalaya, when briefly pulsed in a food processor it becomes self-binding. There is no need to add an egg. Use it to stuff vegetables, seafood, pork chops, and chicken. It is my favorite stuffing for bell peppers.

Crunchy Leftover Jambalaya Salad

As a child, I loved a cold jambalaya sandwich with mayo on old-fashioned white bread. This salad on a croissant is my grown-up version. Any type of leftover jambalaya can be used, but my favorite is chicken and sausage. This salad is a cross between a rice salad and a Chinese chicken salad. The celery, water chestnuts, and almonds give it a nice crunch, and the olives and artichokes add a pleasant tanginess.

1/4 tsp. curry powder
1/2 cup mayonnaise
1 1/2 cups cold leftover jambalaya
8-oz can water chestnuts, drained,*
  finely chopped
14-oz. can quartered artichoke
  hearts, drained,* chopped

2 green onions, sliced
2 celery stalks, chopped
4 stuffed olives, chopped
1/4 cup sliced almonds, toasted

Mix curry powder into mayonnaise. Set aside.

In a mixing bowl, combine all other ingredients. Stir in curry mayo until well blended. Chill for a few hours or overnight before serving.

Makes 4 cups

*Reserve liquid from water chestnuts and artichoke hearts. The artichoke juice can be added as needed to adjust jambalaya salad to desired consistency. The reserved liquids can also be used to make salad dressing or to add flavor to hummus, pesto, or a stir fry.

TO COOK IS TO CREATE: Have leftover rotisserie chicken? Add it to this recipe. Have a tomato? Chop it and add it. Not a lover of curry powder? Try paprika, ground ginger, or cumin powder. No almonds? Use pecans. No olives? Use pimentos. For crunch, you can substitute canned Chinese vegetables, chopped bell peppers, or shredded carrots. I like adding thinly shredded cabbage for a change. If omitting artichoke hearts, give the salad a little squeeze of lemon. Not a salad-sandwich fan? Stuff this into a tomato or serve over lettuce. No leftover jambalaya? Use wild rice or leftover dirty rice.

Leftover Jambalaya Muffins

I love serving these muffins with gumbo, but if you want to simply snack away on them, then the sweet-'n'-spicy dipping sauce is the way to go.

½ cup leftover jambalaya
½ cup milk
1 egg, beaten
2½ tbsp. butter, melted
¾ cup flour, sifted
1 tsp. sugar
¼ tsp. salt

¼ tsp. garlic powder
1½ tsp. baking powder

For the Sauce:
2 tbsp. honey
2 tbsp. chili sauce
½ tsp. crushed red pepper flakes

Preheat oven to 400 degrees.

Dice any large pieces of meat, poultry, or seafood in the jambalaya. Whisk jambalaya, milk, egg, and butter until well blended.

Sift in flour, sugar, salt, garlic powder, and baking powder. Mix to combine, forming a batter.

Drop mixture by tablespoons into each well of a lightly greased mini muffin tin. (You will have enough batter for 16 muffins.) Bake for 12-15 minutes or until a toothpick comes out clean.

To make the sauce, mix the honey, chili sauce, and red pepper flakes until well blended. Serve muffins with the sauce.

Refrigerate leftovers. To reheat muffins, wrap in foil and bake at 350 degrees for 10 minutes.

Makes 16 mini muffins

TO COOK IS TO CREATE: No leftover jambalaya? Use dirty rice. Add onion powder, Creole seasoning, or cayenne to the batter. Other sauces or spreads to consider are pepper jelly, remoulade, cocktail sauce, bacon jam, or a flavored butter. Have leftover white or red beans? Serve as a hot and hearty dipping sauce for the muffins.

Cajun Stuffed Fried Okra

Want to get the kids to try okra? Serve up these fried ones filled with leftover jambalaya and with ranch dressing for dipping instead of the squeeze of lime. No worries about using the beer; considering the high heat and the cooking time, the alcohol will burn off.

$\frac{1}{2}$ cup leftover jambalaya
$\frac{1}{2}$ cup cornmeal
$\frac{1}{2}$ cup self-rising flour
1 tsp. Creole seasoning

8 oz. dark beer
12 fresh okra pods, rinsed, dried
Oil for frying
Juice of half a lime

Place leftover jambalaya in a mini food processor. Pulse until mixture begins to stick together.

In a bowl, mix cornmeal, flour, and Creole seasoning. Slowly whisk in beer. Let sit for 30 minutes.

Using a paring knife, split each okra down middle, and stuff with 1 tsp. leftover jambalaya. Press okra around stuffing to seal the okra.

Heat oil to 350 degrees. Holding by the stem, dip each okra into beer batter. Gently drop into oil. Fry for 5 minutes or until golden brown.

Drain on paper towels. Squeeze stuffed okra with lime before serving.

Tiny Tidbit: Use leftover jambalaya to stuff and fry jalapeno peppers!

Fried Jambalaya Pepper Jack Balls

I absolutely love cheese-filled boudin balls and never miss an opportunity to buy some. These fried leftover-jambalaya balls filled with pepper jack cheese remind me of some of the best cheese-filled boudin balls I have had around Louisiana.

1 cup leftover jambalaya
6 small cubes pepper jack cheese
1 cup all-purpose flour
1 tsp. Creole seasoning
1 egg

1 tsp. Louisiana hot sauce
1 tbsp. water
1 cup Italian breadcrumbs
Oil for frying

Place leftover jambalaya in a mini food processor. Pulse until mixture begins to stick together.

Divide mixture into 6 equal portions. Using moistened hands, form mixture into golf-ball-sized balls. Press 1 cube pepper jack cheese into each ball and press to seal it in.

In a small bowl, mix the flour with the Creole seasoning. Set aside.

In another small bowl, whisk the egg, hot sauce, and water. Set aside.

Add breadcrumbs to another small bowl.

With breading station set up, dip 1 ball into seasoned flour, then egg, letting excess drip off. Then roll in breadcrumbs. Repeat for remaining balls.

Set balls onto a parchment-lined plate. Chill for at least 1 hour or up to overnight.

Heat oil in a deep fryer or large saucepan to 350 degrees. Fry balls until brown and crispy, about $1\frac{1}{2}$ to 2 minutes.

Makes 6 balls

Jambalaya Scotch Eggs with Malt Vinegar Sauce

Belly up to the bar for this pub fare, which pairs nicely with a tall cold beer. A traditional Scotch egg is a hardboiled egg wrapped in sausage meat, rolled in breadcrumbs, and fried. This "Scotch egg" took a trip to Louisiana and substitutes leftover jambalaya for the sausage meat. These are great served over shredded cabbage.

½ cup leftover jambalaya
2 large hardboiled eggs, peeled
½ cup all-purpose flour
1 tsp. Creole seasoning
½ cup chicken stock

½ cup minced saltines
Oil for frying
¼ cup mayonnaise
¼ cup Creole mustard
1 tbsp. malt vinegar

Place leftover jambalaya in a mini food processor. Pulse until mixture begins to stick together.

Divide mixture into 2 equal portions. Take 1 portion and flatten in the palm of your hand. Lay 1 egg on top and wrap mixture around entire egg. Seal completely. Repeat with remaining mixture and egg.

Set up a breading station. Add flour and seasoning to one bowl, stock to another and saltines to the third bowl.

Dip jambalaya covered eggs into flour, then stock, and saltines, coating all sides.

Chill eggs for 30 minutes.

Heat oil to 350 degrees. Using a slotted spoon, lower eggs into oil. Fry for 3½-4 minutes.

In a small bowl, whisk together mayonnaise and mustard. Slowly whisk in malt vinegar.

Serve sauce on side for dipping.

Makes 2 large eggs

Tiny Tidbit: Use leftover jambalaya when making deviled eggs.

Jambalaya Soup

This hearty soup is as versatile as jambalaya itself. It utilizes frozen vegetables and seasonings, making it quick and easy to fix. Other canned vegetables can also be added, turning this into a pantry soup.

1 tsp. olive oil
2 cups frozen chopped seasoning
   (green pepper, onion, celery)
2 cloves garlic, minced
10 oz. can diced tomatoes and green
   chilies

1 cup leftover jambalaya
4 cups chicken stock
1 bay leaf
1 1/2 cups frozen vegetables, such as
   corn and okra

In a stockpot that has a cover, over medium-high heat, add olive oil. Sauté seasoning and garlic, uncovered, for 5 minutes. Stir in tomatoes and jambalaya. Cook for 2 minutes.

Slowly stir in the chicken stock, scraping bottom of pot to loosen any brown bits. Add bay leaf. Raise heat and bring mixture just to a boil.

Reduce heat to low. Cover and simmer for 15 minutes.

Add vegetables. Cover and cook an additional 15 minutes. Remove bay leaf before serving.

Serves 4

TO COOK IS TO CREATE: Have other leftovers, such as ham, beans, or chicken? Throw them in. Also, think about how other stocks could enhance the flavor. For example, for a vegetable jambalaya use a vegetable or corncob stock, and for a seafood jambalaya use a seafood or beef stock. What other vegetables could you add? Sliced carrots, sliced yellow squash, sliced zucchini, cubed eggplant, or canned lima beans are nice additions. Just remember to adjust the cooking times for canned, fresh, or frozen vegetables.

JAMBALAYA NACHOS

A simple addition of onions, bell peppers, chili powder, and tomato paste transports leftover jambalaya south of the Border. I use this jambalaya mixture not only for nachos but also tacos, quesadillas, and burritos.

1 tsp. olive oil
1 onion, chopped
1 yellow bell pepper, chopped
1 red bell pepper, chopped
1 clove garlic, minced
2 tsp. chili powder
$1/4$ cup water

1 cup leftover jambalaya
1 tbsp. tomato paste
Corn tortilla chips
2 cups grated cheddar and
   Monterey Jack cheese
Jalapeno slices, for topping
Sour cream (optional)

Preheat oven to 350 degrees.

In a skillet, over medium heat, heat olive oil. Add onions, bell peppers, and garlic. Sauté for 5 minutes.

Add the chili powder. Stir for 1 minute to toast seasoning.

Add water to pan, and scrape up any brown bits.

Chop any large pieces of meat, poultry, or seafood in the leftover jambalaya, then add the jambalaya and tomato paste to the pan. Stir well. Reduce heat to low and simmer for 5 minutes.

Spread tortilla chips on a parchment-lined baking sheet. Spoon the jambalaya mixture over the chips. Top with cheese.

Bake until cheese is melted, about 5 minutes.

Top nachos with jalapeno slices and sour cream, if desired.

Makes 1 large plate for sharing

Leftover Jambalaya Grilled Cheese

I love grilled cheese sandwiches. A simple childhood pleasure is relived each time the gooey cheese pulls apart. I can almost hear my mom warning me that it might be too hot, but isn't pulling the sandwich apart with the hot cheese the best part?

½ cup leftover jambalaya
1 tsp. olive oil
4 slices sourdough bread
2 tbsp. mayonnaise

1 tbsp. unsalted butter
2 slices Muenster cheese
2 tbsp. pepper jelly
2 slices Monterey Jack

Place leftover jambalaya in a mini food processor. Pulse until mixture begins to stick together. Divide mixture in half and form into 2 patties.

In a skillet, over medium heat, add olive oil. Add patties and cook for 1 minute on each side. Remove from skillet.

Lay out slices of bread and spread mayonnaise over top of each slice.

In the skillet, over medium heat, add butter. When melted, add 2 bread slices, mayonnaise side down. Top each with 1 slice Muenster cheese, 1 tbsp. pepper jelly, 1 jambalaya patty, 1 slice Monterey Jack, and remaining bread slice, mayonnaise side up. Gently press each with a spatula.

Cook until cheese is melted and bread is toasted, about 3 minutes per side. Slice in half diagonally and serve.

Makes 2 sandwiches

Tiny Tidbit: Try a leftover jambalaya patty on your favorite sandwich. It's great on a BLT, for example.

Jambalaya Sauce

Use this quick sauce to top fried catfish (my favorite); blackened fish; fried, blackened, or baked chicken; or even omelettes or pasta.

1/2 cup leftover jambalaya
1/4 cup diced tomatoes, about 1
    large Roma tomato
2/3 cup heavy cream

1/2 tsp. Creole seasoning
1-2 dashes Louisiana hot sauce
1 green onion, sliced

Chop any large pieces of meat, poultry, or seafood in the jambalaya. In a saucepan, over medium-low heat, add leftover jambalaya and tomatoes. Cook until heated through, about 5 minutes.

Stir in cream, seasoning, and hot sauce. Continue stirring for 3 minutes until smooth and slightly thickened. (Sauce will thicken more upon standing.)

Remove from heat. Stir in green onions. Serve sauce over desired dish.

Makes 1/2 cup sauce

Tiny Tidbit: Like biscuits and gravy? Serve this sauce over split biscuits.

Bacon-Wrapped Jambalaya-Stuffed Fish

Leftover jambalaya makes such an easy stuffing, and the addition of bacon makes the stuffed fish even better. I like to serve this fish over a bed of sautéed spinach.

1 cup leftover jambalaya
8 slices bacon
4 catfish fillets (6 oz. each)
1 tbsp. lemon juice

1 tsp. lemon pepper
Olive oil
2 tbsp. Creole mustard

Preheat oven to 375 degrees.

Place leftover jambalaya in a food processor. Pulse until mixture begins to stick together. Set aside.

On a cutting board, lay out bacon slices in pairs, with each pair slightly overlapping.

Rinse fish, and pat dry. Sprinkle fish with lemon juice and lemon pepper. Lay each fillet, lengthwise, onto a pair of bacon slices.

Mound ¼ cup jambalaya on the end of each fillet. Roll fillets and bacon up tightly.

Line a baking sheet with parchment and top with a baking rack. Brush or spray rack with olive oil. Place bacon-wrapped fish, seam side down, on baking rack.

Bake for 30 minutes.

Brush Creole mustard onto each bacon-wrapped bundle. Broil for 2 minutes.

Serves 4

Jambalaya Eggplant Casserole

I love eggplant, and I love this "a little goes a long way" recipe. Less than 2 cups of leftover jambalaya and a few ingredients make a large casserole to share with family and friends.

1 lb. ground beef
1 onion, chopped
1 bell pepper, chopped
2 celery stalks, chopped
2 cloves garlic, minced
1 tsp. Creole seasoning
$\frac{1}{2}$ tsp. dry mustard

1 large eggplant, cubed
2 cans (14.5 oz. each) tomatoes
    and okra
1 $\frac{1}{2}$ cups leftover jambalaya
$\frac{3}{4}$ cup breadcrumbs
$\frac{1}{2}$ cup grated Parmesan cheese

Preheat oven to 350 degrees.

In a large skillet that has a lid, over medium-high heat, brown the beef and drain.

Reduce heat to medium. Add onion, bell pepper, celery, and garlic, and sauté for 5 minutes.

Add the Creole seasoning and dry mustard. Stir in the eggplant and tomatoes and okra. Cover. Reduce heat to low and cook for 10 minutes.

Stir in leftover jambalaya and remove from heat.

Spoon mixture into a 9x13 casserole dish. Top with breadcrumbs and Parmesan cheese. Cover with foil.

Bake on middle rack for 20 minutes. Remove foil. Bake an additional 10 minutes.

Serves 6-8

Tiny Tidbit: Use leftover jambalaya to make a quick stir fry or fried rice.

Onion Skin Salt

Here is an ingenious use for the skins that will be left over anytime you use an onion.

Preheat oven to 150 degrees. Lay onion-skin pieces on a parchment-lined baking sheet. Oven dry for 2 hours.

Place dried skin in a food processor. Mince. Add ground Mediterranean sea salt. Pulse until blended.

Store in airtight container. Use within 1 month.

ETOUFFÉE

Etouffée is a fancy French word meaning smothered. In Louisiana, we love to "smother" just about anything to make an étouffée: chicken, sausage, seafood, vegetables, and even alligator. The "holy trinity" of bell pepper, celery, and onion is added, along with tons of butter. The étouffée—or "gravy," as it is lovingly called in some parts—is then served over rice as a rich delicacy.

Wondering what the difference is between an étouffée and a "Creole," such as a chicken, shrimp, or crawfish Creole? Although they are closely related, they have a few key distinctions. Etouffée uses a roux for a base, and Creoles use tomatoes as a base. Etouffée is usually thick, like a gravy, while Creoles are a bit thinner. Etouffées are darker, with an orange hue, and Creoles are redder due to the tomatoes.

In the following recipes, leftover étouffée can easily be replaced with a leftover Creole.

Etouffée French Bread Pizza

Leftover étouffée blended with cream cheese makes a flavorful base for your favorite pizza toppings or leftover bits you may have in the fridge. I love using fresh spinach and black olives with seafood étouffée, but any kind of étouffée will work, as will shrimp or chicken Creole.

4 oz. cream cheese, softened
1 clove garlic, minced
1 cup leftover étouffée
1 small loaf French bread (12 in.) or
    4 pistolettes

1 cup grated cheddar or Colby and
    Monterey Jack cheese
Toppings of your choice

Preheat oven to 375 degrees.

Using a rubber spatula, stir cream cheese, garlic, and leftover étouffée together until well blended.

Cut French bread or pistolettes in half lengthwise. Spread mixture onto bread halves. Top each with cheese and desired toppings.

Bake for 12-15 minutes or until cheese is melted.

Serves 4

Tiny Tidbit: Use leftover crawfish étouffée to top a hot dog.

Leftover Crawfish Etouffée Enchiladas

This dish was inspired by my love of enchiladas smothered in sour cream sauce. Using leftover étouffée in and on top of these enchiladas ensures that every bite is full of flavor. I love this with crawfish étouffée, but leftover shrimp étouffée or even shrimp or crawfish Creole can be substituted. For a change, sometimes I like to serve the hot enchiladas on shredded lettuce.

Nonstick cooking or olive oil spray
8.75 oz. can corn, drained, or 1 cup frozen corn, thawed
1 cup leftover étouffée, divided
½ cup cooked rice
1 cup grated cheese (Queso, Monterey Jack, cheddar, or a blend)

¼ lb. crawfish tails, crabmeat, or cooked diced shrimp (optional)
12 corn tortillas (6 in., white or yellow)
4 oz. can diced green chiles
¼ cup sour cream
1 cup grated cheese for topping (optional)

Preheat oven to 350 degrees. Lightly spray a 9x13 casserole dish with nonstick cooking or olive oil spray.

In a bowl, add corn, ½ cup étouffée, rice, 1 cup cheese, and other seafood, if using. Mix well. Set aside.

In a nonstick skillet, over medium heat, warm tortillas for 10-15 seconds per side. Keep warm in a tortilla warmer or dish towel.

Place 2 tbsp. crawfish mixture in a line down center of 1 tortilla. Tuck over 1 side and roll filled tortilla into a cigar shape. Place seam side down in greased casserole dish. Repeat with remaining tortillas.

In a small saucepan, add remaining ½ cup étouffée and diced green chiles. Simmer for 5 minutes, stirring occasionally. Remove from heat. Stir in sour cream.

Pour sauce over enchiladas. Top with cheese, if desired. Bake for 20 minutes.

Makes 12 enchiladas

TO COOK IS TO CREATE: What else could you add to the filling? Try sautéed spinach, sautéed mushrooms, black beans, shredded carrots, diced zucchini, chopped tomatillos, chopped roasted poblano peppers, or sliced jalapenos. No white rice? Use cooked quinoa, yellow, wild, or brown rice. No seafood? Substitute leftover rotisserie chicken, cooked smoked sausage, or chorizo. If you like black olives, add some. Not a cheese fan? Top the enchiladas with chopped tomatoes, avocados or guacamole, or additional sour cream.

Easy Etouffée Baked Fish

Have leftover étouffée and rice? Then simply add a few more ingredients for an easy dinner for four. Having a dinner party? This recipe makes a nice presentation with one fish fillet per person baked in individual oval casserole dishes. Boneless, skinless chicken breasts can be substituted for fish. Simply brown in a little olive oil before adding to the casserole.

Butter, softened
1 cup leftover rice
1 zucchini, sliced
1 onion, thinly sliced

4 catfish fillets (6 oz. each)
2 tsp. Creole seasoning
1½ cups leftover étouffée

Preheat oven to 350 degrees. Butter a 2-3-qt.-sized casserole dish, one that is just big enough so fish will not overlap.

Spread rice in a thin layer on bottom, and top with sliced zucchini and onions.

Rinse fish, and pat dry. Sprinkle fish with seasoning and place onto onion slices.

Spread leftover étouffée over fish. Cover with foil and bake for 30 minutes.

Remove foil and bake an additional 5 minutes.

Serves 4

Tiny Tidbit: Use leftover étouffée to stuff baked potatoes.

Louisiana Poached Catfish

Full confession: I love to cook but I hate doing dishes. This one-pot recipe saves the day when it is my turn to clean the kitchen. The catfish is cooked, or poached, by simmering in a small amount of wine and leftover étouffée. The beauty of this recipe is that it also works well with leftover Creoles, bisques, or stews. The fish can be served over a bed of rice, grits, or pasta.

$\frac{1}{2}$ **tbsp. olive oil**
1 bell pepper, sliced
1 onion, sliced

1 cup leftover étouffée
$\frac{1}{2}$ **cup white wine or water**
2 large or 4 small catfish fillets

In a skillet that has a lid, over medium heat, add olive oil. Sauté bell pepper and onion for 5 minutes.

Add étouffée along with wine or water. Raise heat to high. Bring to a boil.

Rinse and dry fish, then add to skillet. Cover. Reduce heat to low. Simmer for 10 minutes or until fish flakes easily with a fork.

Remove fish to a plate. Return heat to high and bring mixture back to a boil. Stir and cook until reduced, 2-3 minutes. Serve sauce over fish.

Serves 2-4

TO COOK IS TO CREATE: What other stews or soups would be good in this dish? Try a loaded potato soup. What else could you add instead of the onions and bell peppers? Think of any vegetable that would add flavor when steamed, such as eggplant, yellow squash, or zucchini.

Leftover Etouffée Shrimp Marinara

Need a quick weeknight meal? This pasta dish comes together in under 30 minutes, but no one will be able to guess. It may have a short cooking time but it's certainly not short on flavor.

16 oz. farfalle (bowtie) pasta
1 tsp. olive oil
8 oz. smoked sausage, chopped
1 large yellow onion, chopped
1 green bell pepper, chopped
2 cloves garlic, minced
4 oz. red wine
28 oz. can crushed tomatoes

1 tsp. dried oregano
$\frac{1}{2}$ tsp. crushed red pepper flakes
1 tsp. sugar
1 cup leftover étouffée
1 lb. medium (41-50 ct.) peeled, deveined shrimp
1 tbsp. unsalted butter
Fresh basil leaves (optional)

Cook pasta according to package instructions.

In a stockpot, over medium heat, add olive oil. Add sausage, onion, pepper, and garlic. Sauté for 5 minutes.

Stir in wine, scraping up any brown bits from bottom of pot, then stir in tomatoes, oregano, pepper flakes, and sugar. Bring mixture to a boil.

Add leftover étouffée. Reduce heat to low. Cover and simmer for 15 minutes.

Stir shrimp into the simmering sauce. Cook for 5 minutes or until shrimp turn pink.

Remove from heat. Stir in butter. Serve over drained pasta. Cut fresh basil into strips and sprinkle over dish, if desired.

Serves 4

TO COOK IS TO CREATE: No shrimp? Use crawfish tails. No smoked sausage? Use leftover rotisserie chicken or cooked ham. You can also substitute your favorite shaped pasta for the bowties. Use 1 tbsp. fresh oregano, if you have it. Not a pepper fan? Omit the red pepper flakes. But if you like it spicy, add a can of diced green chiles.

Tiny Tidbit: If you have leftover cooked shaped pasta, make a quick snack by simply frying it until crisp, then tossing with your favorite seasonings and/or toppings. I love Italian seasoning with garlic powder and Parmesan cheese.

GUMBO

"First you make a roux . . ." are like the words, "Once upon a time. . . ." They are the start of a great story with a beautiful ending—gumbo! Everybody has their own way of preparing it, usually from a family recipe passed down for generations. Gumbo is a true "melting pot" of flavors. It is thought to have originated in South Louisiana during the eighteenth century. Its fame increased in the 1970s, when seafood gumbo was added to the U.S. Senate's cafeteria menu in honor of Louisiana senator Allen Ellender, of Houma, who served for thirty-five years and was known for his Cajun cooking.

We do love our gumbo here in Louisiana and in fact sometimes even judge the weather by it. "This is gumbo weather" is a legit weather report for a cold day. I know that leftover gumbo is a rarity, but if you find you only have one cup of gumbo left and want to share it with your family, here are some recipes. However, if you choose to tuck that last cup of gumbo behind everything in the fridge and selfishly save it for yourself, your secret is safe with me.

When storing gumbo and rice, store them separately, to get the most use out of the leftovers.

Tiny Tidbit: Need a quick way to reheat rice? Simply put into a strainer in the sink, and run hot water over it until heated through.

LAYERED GUMBO DIP

I like to serve this dip when friends and family visit from out of town in the heat of summer. It gives them the taste of gumbo in one bite and gives me a good excuse to use some leftover gumbo from the freezer.

½ cup leftover rice
¼ tsp. Worcestershire sauce
4 oz. cream cheese
Louisiana hot sauce, to taste

1 small tomato, chopped
½ cup leftover gumbo
2 pickled okra pods, sliced (optional)
Crackers or toast points for serving

Preheat oven to 350 degrees.

In a small saucepan, over medium heat, add rice, Worcestershire sauce, cream cheese, and hot sauce. Stir until cheese is melted. Spread mixture onto the bottom of a small au gratin or casserole dish.

Top mixture with chopped tomato and leftover gumbo.

Cover with foil and bake for 20 minutes. Remove foil. Bake an additional 8-10 minutes or until bubbly.

Top with pickled okra slices, if desired. Serve with crackers or toast points.

Serves 4

Leftover Gumbo Sloppy Joes

This is my hubby's absolute favorite. That's no surprise, considering it is a combination of two of his favorite dishes—gumbo and hamburgers. This recipe is a cost-effective way to feed your family with just one cup of leftover gumbo.

1 tsp. olive oil
1 onion, chopped
1 lb. ground beef
1 clove garlic, minced
1 cup leftover gumbo

1 tomato, chopped
1 tsp. dry mustard
Louisiana hot sauce, to taste
6 pistolettes, split
2 tbsp. butter, melted

In a large skillet, over medium-high heat, add olive oil and onions. Sauté for 2 minutes.

Add the ground beef, breaking apart into crumbles as it browns. Cook for 8 minutes or until no longer pink. Drain and return to skillet.

Add garlic, gumbo, tomatoes, dry mustard, and hot sauce. Reduce heat to low. Simmer for 20 minutes, stirring occasionally.

Heat oven to 350 degrees.

Spread open pistolettes and brush cut sides with melted butter. Place buttered side down on a baking sheet lined with parchment paper. Bake for 5 minutes.

Serve gumbo sloppy joe mixture in pistolettes.

TO COOK IS TO CREATE: Does your leftover gumbo include okra or other vegetables? If not, add frozen sliced okra or corn kernels during the last 10 minutes of simmering. Like it spicy? Add a can of diced tomatoes and green chilies instead of the tomato, and serve on jalapeno cheddar rolls. Are you a bacon lover? Add cooked crumbled bacon to the mixture before serving.

Gumbo Casserole

This is a remake of a pork-chop casserole that has been around for years. You know the one: cream of mushroom soup, potatoes, and lots and lots of cheese. In fact, I chuckle to myself when I remember making the casserole in college and my roommates and I thinking it was gourmet. At least it was better than the cafeteria! This casserole uses leftover gumbo in place of the mushroom soup, but I do add mushrooms. I guess you can say I am a bit nostalgic for old recipes. I cannot eat gumbo without saltine crackers, so I use them as a crispy topping.

4 boneless, center cut pork chops
Salt and freshly ground pepper
1 tbsp. olive oil
1 large baking potato, thinly sliced
1 medium onion, thinly sliced
1 red bell pepper, chopped

8 oz. white button mushrooms, sliced
10 oz. frozen green peas
1 cup leftover gumbo
10 saltine crackers, crushed

Pat pork chops dry. Season with salt and pepper.

In a 12-in. skillet, over medium-high heat, add olive oil. Place pork chops in oil and sear for 2 minutes on each side.

Preheat oven to 350 degrees.

Arrange the potatoes in the bottom of a 9x13 casserole dish, overlapping if necessary. Add onion slices, bell pepper, mushrooms, and peas.

Add the browned pork chops onto vegetables.

Pour gumbo on top of casserole, and spread to cover.

Cover casserole with foil. Bake for 30 minutes. Uncover. Bake an additional 30 minutes.

Add crushed crackers to top and bake for 5 minutes.

TO COOK IS TO CREATE: Is cornbread or a biscuit your favorite side when enjoying gumbo? If so, just add some sliced biscuits, or biscuit dough or cornbread batter, to the top of the casserole the last 30 minutes. No frozen peas? Use any frozen vegetables you have on hand. You can also substitute breadcrumbs or crushed potato chips for the saltine crackers.

Tiny Tidbit: Serve leftover gumbo over grits.

Louisiana Seafood Saturday Night

From Boils to Fried Seafood

A famous song says, "There ain't nothing like a Louisiana Saturday night." I love Saturdays spent with family and friends indulging in all the best that Louisiana has to offer. Whether it is standing around an outdoor table sharing the first batch of hot boiled crawfish poured from the pot, handing around a plate of boiled shrimp, or sharing an enormous fried seafood platter, it is all about passing a good time together. Add a little Cajun music, and *"laissez les bons temps rouler!"* Let the good times roll!

For me, there's nothing like a Louisiana Saturday crawfish boil. I can barely sleep the night before a crawfish boil. Just the thought of hearing the boiling pot rumble gets me excited. I love everything about it . . . well, almost everything. I never sign up for the job of dropping the live crawfish into the pot, but I am the first to volunteer to get them out! Crawfish boils are popular social events, with a lot of standing, eating, drinking, and talking. In fact, I don't think I have ever been to a large crawfish boil where there were seats around a table. It is part of the experience to stand in your spot waiting for the delightful aroma of the hot spicy crawfish being poured down the center of the table. If you happen to be in just the right spot, you can even get a free steam facial! At smaller gatherings, like at home, boiled crawfish are served on newspaper-covered tables and enjoyed sitting down with an ice bucket of cold beer close by. Whether you are standing or sitting, once the crawfish are served, there are no rules. Just eat . . . and I can eat!

When I was in the eighth grade, I won a crawfish eating contest—and I was the only girl! I am happy to say I still have some of my winning moves. I have been told I am an endurance crawfish eater because I am usually one of the last eating at the table. Sometimes, however, I manage to save some of the goodies from the boil for my favorite leftover-crawfish recipes. The boiler pots usually don't get boiling without potatoes, corn, sausage or boudin, onions, and garlic, but eggs, artichokes, asparagus, and mushrooms are fair game also, and the same goes for the pots boiling with shrimp or crabs, too.

Heads and shells from boiled crawfish and shrimp, and crab shells, can be used to make flavored butters. Add the shells and heads to a bag and use a rubber mallet to crush them. This is a great way to work out any frustrations! Then simply add the crushed shells to the top of a double boiler, along with $\frac{1}{4}$ cup butter per pound of heads and shells. Heat over medium low for 15 minutes, stirring frequently. Add some fresh herbs or seasonings, and continue to cook for 15 minutes. Strain and let cool. Freeze shell butter for use in chowders or sauces or as a steak topping.

No pots boiling near you on a Saturday? Then you can bet there are outdoor fryers busy frying up the catch of the day or seafood restaurants serving up everything fried to eager customers waiting for their first crispy bite. Nowadays, seafood platter portions are way too big but perfect for sharing and for saving the leftovers. That means the French fries, too.

Convection ovens and air fryers make re-crisping leftover fried food easier than ever. But a few of my leftover seafood favorites are cold fried shrimp salad, cold fried catfish over cheese grits, and cold fried oysters dropped onto some hot spinach and artichoke dip.

Stirring up the fun, boiled crawfish almost done.

Leftover Crawfish Boil Fritters with Creamed Corn Sauce

This recipe turns the leftover crawfish tails, potatoes, garlic, and sausage into fritters, but not just any fritters—think tater tot meets hushpuppy. The leftover corn from the boil makes a rich, creamy sauce to serve alongside. These fritters can also be made into patties and pan fried, if preferred.

1 link leftover boiled sausage, chopped
1 small onion, chopped
1 large or 3-4 small leftover boiled potatoes, cubed
2 leftover boiled cloves garlic, peeled
1 cup leftover peeled crawfish tails*
1 egg, beaten

1 tsp. Worcestershire sauce
Oil for frying
1 tbsp. butter
1 tbsp. flour
$\frac{1}{4}$ tsp. white pepper
$\frac{1}{2}$ cup heavy cream
Kernels from 2 leftover boiled corncob sections**

For the fritters, add sausage and onion to a food processor. Pulse until minced.

Add potatoes and garlic. Pulse a few times.

Add crawfish tails, and pulse just until chopped fine. Scrape mixture into a bowl.

To the bowl, add the beaten egg and Worcestershire sauce. Mix all ingredients together well. Using moistened hands, grab the crawfish mixture by heaping tablespoons and roll into balls.

Put balls onto a plate lined with parchment paper and chill for 30 minutes.

In a heavy-bottomed pot or deep fryer, heat oil to 350 degrees. Deep fry balls for 2-3 minutes or until golden brown. Drain on paper towels.

For the sauce, melt butter in a small saucepan over medium heat. Blend in flour, white pepper, cream, and corn kernels. Stir constantly until desired thickness.

Serve fritters with sauce.

Makes 10 fritters

*Leftover boiled shrimp can be substituted.

**Leftover boiled corncobs can also be used to make corncob stock.

Cheesy Crawfish Rolls

My two loves united—crawfish and cheese! This recipe is a bit on the rich side but well worth the splurge.

⅓ cup whipped cream cheese
1 cup grated cheddar cheese
1 cup grated Monterey Jack cheese
⅓ cup mayonnaise
½ tsp. Creole seasoning
2 tbsp. diced pimentos
1 tsp. grated onion

2 green onions, sliced
Black pepper
Louisiana hot sauce, to taste
¾-1 cup leftover peeled crawfish tails
6 pistolettes

Preheat oven to 400 degrees.

Using a hand mixer, beat cream cheese until fluffy. Add remaining ingredients, except for crawfish and pistolettes, and beat until well blended. Fold in crawfish.

Split pistolettes down center at the top, taking care not to cut all the way through. Use fingers to press insides, forming a hollow. Add cheese mixture to each hollow. Wrap each roll tightly in parchment paper.

Bake directly on middle oven rack for 10-12 minutes.

Tiny Tidbit: No pistolettes? Use the cheesy crawfish mixture as a filling for stuffed baked potatoes!

"Pig in a Cloud" Stuffed Sausage Bread with Crawfish Buttercream Sauce and Five-Pepper Jelly

Don't let the length of this recipe keep you away from making this bread. If you love the famous stuffed breads found around Louisiana, then you will love this one, too. Wondering why I call it "Pig in a Cloud"? The richness of the crawfish buttercream sauce, the kick from the pepper jelly, and the crunch from the sausage-filled fried bread all in one bite are heavenly to me.

1 roll bulk pork sausage, hot or mild
2 eggs, lightly beaten, divided
1/3 cup breadcrumbs
1 small onion, diced
1 bell pepper, diced
1 clove garlic, minced
6 pistolettes
1 tsp. water
2 cups all-purpose flour
2 tsp. Creole seasoning
Oil for frying

For the Crawfish Buttercream Sauce:
3 tbsp. unsalted butter, divided
8 oz. leftover peeled crawfish tails
1/2 tsp. cumin
1/2 tsp. dry mustard
1/2 tsp. paprika
1 tsp. blackened seasoning
1 1/2 cups heavy cream
1/4 cup thinly sliced green onions

For the Five-Pepper Jelly:
6 oz. white vinegar
6 oz. corn syrup
1 small green bell pepper, chopped
1 small red bell pepper, chopped
1 small orange bell pepper, chopped
1 small yellow bell pepper, chopped
1/4 tsp. crushed red pepper flakes
    (optional)
Pinch of salt

Preheat oven to 350 degrees.

In a bowl, combine sausage, 1 beaten egg, breadcrumbs, onions, peppers, and garlic. Divide mixture into 6 equal portions. Form portions into 6 logs.

Arrange logs on a rack over a baking sheet. Bake for 20 minutes or until cooked through.

Cut out a small piece on one end of each pistolette; save cut pieces. Use fingers to press around inside each pistolette, making a hollow. Push sausage into breads. Firmly push cut pieces back into breads.

In a bowl, mix the remaining beaten egg with water and in another, mix flour with Creole seasoning. Dip breads into egg wash, then into seasoned flour.

In a heavy-bottomed pot or deep fryer, heat oil to 350 degrees. Deep fry pistolettes for 2 minutes or until lightly browned.

To make the Crawfish Buttercream Sauce, heat saucepan over medium heat. Melt 2 tbsp. butter. When melted, add crawfish, cumin, mustard, paprika, and blackened seasoning. Cook for 2 minutes.

Add cream and bring mixture to a boil. Stir, reduce heat to low, and simmer for 3 minutes. Remove from heat. Stir in remaining butter and green onions.

To make the Five-Pepper Jelly, in a small saucepan over medium-high heat, reduce vinegar and corn syrup until it coats the back of a spoon. Add peppers and pepper flakes, if desired. Reduce heat and cook until peppers are soft. Add pinch of salt. Let cool.

Serve stuffed bread with Crawfish Buttercream Sauce topped with Five-Pepper Jelly.

Makes 6 sausage breads

TO COOK IS TO CREATE: Have smoked sausage or leftover cooked meatloaf or hamburgers? Mince and use in place of the bulk sausage to save some time. Want to go meat free? Use vegetables such as broccoli, or spinach and cheese, or a blend of mushrooms. Don't want to deep fry? No problem. Skip the egg wash and breading, and enjoy the pistolettes simply warmed in the oven. If you do this and want an extra layer of flavor, brush the bread with melted butter and sprinkle with seasonings or cheese. No crawfish for the buttercream sauce? Substitute cooked shrimp or crabmeat. And if you're not in the mood for stuffed bread, enjoy the sauce over blackened chicken or fish.

Boiler Pot Garlic Sticky Chicken

The honey glaze makes my fingers sticky from eating this chicken. And I love garlic, especially with the added "bite" of being boiled with spicy seasonings. If I have any leftover chicken from this recipe, I enjoy it in a salad.

4 leftover boiled cloves garlic, peeled
2 tbsp. honey
2 tbsp. low-sodium soy sauce
1 tsp. ground ginger
1 tsp. Chinese five-spice powder
1 lb. boneless, skinless chicken thighs
Olive oil spray

Preheat oven to 350 degrees.

Mash garlic cloves. Add to a small bowl, and whisk in honey, soy sauce, ginger, and five-spice powder. Brush mixture onto chicken thighs.

Line the bottom of a broiler pan with parchment for easy cleanup, and spray broiler rack with olive oil. Place chicken thighs onto broiler rack.

Bake for 20 minutes. Turn oven to broil, and broil for 5 minutes for an internal temperature of 165 degrees.

Serves 4

Tiny Tidbit: When boiling water for pasta, throw in a few cloves of garlic. Blend the softened cloves with butter to make garlic bread to serve with the pasta, or use the boiled garlic to make this chicken.

Leftover Potatoes Antipasto Salad

This salad is very versatile. It can be spooned onto a bed of spinach or lettuce, stuffed into a tomato or avocado, or simply served with crackers. The lemony dressing adds a light, refreshing flavor no matter how it is served.

5 small leftover boiled potatoes
1 small lemon, zested and juiced
2 tbsp. olive oil
2 green onions, sliced
1 clove garlic, minced
1 red bell pepper, diced
1 tsp. dried Italian seasoning
1/2 cup chopped leftover boiled
   mushrooms
2.25-oz. can sliced black olives,
   drained*

6-oz. jar artichoke hearts, drained,*
   chopped
14-oz. can hearts of palm, drained,*
   chopped
4 oz. fresh mozzarella, cubed
Leftover boiled shrimp or crawfish,
   peeled
Black pepper

Cube cold leftover potatoes. Put potatoes in large mixing bowl. Add lemon juice and zest. Let sit for 10 minutes.

In a small mixing bowl, stir together olive oil, green onions, garlic, red pepper, and Italian seasoning.

To the potato mixture, add the mushrooms, olives, artichoke hearts, hearts of palm, mozzarella, and leftover boiled shrimp or crawfish.

Add the olive oil mixture. Toss well. Let sit for 30 minutes before serving. Add black pepper.

Serves 4

*The liquids can be used to make salad dressings or marinated mushrooms.

TO COOK IS TO CREATE: Have any other leftovers from a crawfish or shrimp boil? Add them. Can't get enough cheese? Add shredded provolone and Parmesan. If you're not a black olive fan, use green olives or stuffed olives. Lunch meat in the fridge, such as ham or salami, can be sliced and added. Onion fans can include diced red onion or even cocktail onions. Are you an anchovy lover? Add some. Other antipasto items you could toss in include pepperoncini or pickled cauliflower. If not stuffing salad into a tomato, consider adding halved cherry tomatoes.

Zesty Lemon Boiled Shrimp Dip

This recipe satisfies my craving for a hot dip without the heavy cream cheese or sour cream, making it perfect for a hot Louisiana summer day. This dip is also quick to throw together and usually can be made with ingredients already on hand. I use a mixture of black and green olives with pimentos, but use your favorites or even olive salad. This refreshing dip can also be served over rice as a light meal.

½ cup leftover peeled boiled shrimp
1 tbsp. butter
1 tbsp. flour
½ cup white wine
½ lemon, zested and juiced*

¼ cup chopped olives
1 tbsp. chopped fresh herbs (parsley, lemon thyme, thyme, or chives)
1 oz. feta cheese
Black pepper

Add shrimp to a food processor and mince. Set aside.

In a small saucepan, over low heat, melt butter. Stir in flour. Add white wine and lemon juice.

Cook, stirring constantly, until thick and smooth. Add minced shrimp, lemon zest, and olives.

Continue to stir over low heat until heated through. Remove from heat. Stir in fresh herbs.

Crumble feta cheese over top. Season with pepper. Serve with crackers or toast points or over rice for a meal.

Makes 1 cup

*The other half of lemon can be wrapped and frozen. When ready to use, unwrap and place in microwave-safe mug with water. Microwave for 20 seconds. Remove from water and use as usual.

TO COOK IS TO CREATE: No leftover boiled shrimp? Use a can of salmon, pouch of tuna, or leftover cooked fish. No feta cheese? Use shredded Parmesan or mozzarella cheese. Sherry can be substituted for white wine. You could also add minced celery and bell peppers and sliced green onions. Want to stretch this dip and make it a little heavier? Mix in cooked rice. I also have put cooked rice in the bottom of an au gratin dish, topped it with dip and lots of shredded cheese, and broiled it.

Drunken Brunch Shrimp

I love a champagne brunch, and when making this brunch treat, I pour two glasses of champagne: one for the recipe and one for me. This recipe evolved from my love of biscuits and gravy . . . and champagne!

2 tbsp. unsalted butter	$\frac{1}{4}$ tsp. white pepper
1 small onion, diced	1 green onion, sliced
4 oz. champagne	12 leftover boiled shrimp, peeled
$\frac{3}{4}$ cup heavy cream	Biscuits or toasted sourdough

In a small saucepan, over medium heat, add butter and onion. Sauté onion for 5 minutes.

Add champagne, cream, pepper, green onion, and leftover boiled shrimp. Cook, stirring constantly, until thickened. Serve on biscuits or toast.

Serves 2

Tiny Tidbit: Boiled or steamed shrimp can get tough if cooked too long. One trick is to combine boiling and steaming. Pour seasoned boiling water over peeled medium shrimp. Then cover and let stand for 5 minutes.

Sweet and Sour Spicy Shrimp Skillet Slaw

Apple cider vinegar, beer, one Red Delicious apple, and a link of andouille sausage make the base for this hot slaw. The shrimp can be added and warmed, but I enjoy this hot slaw with the cold shrimp. I love the hot slaw even more spooned over a hot dog!

1 tbsp. olive oil
1 small onion, chopped
1 link leftover cooked andouille
   sausage, chopped
4 tbsp. apple cider vinegar
4 tbsp. beer
1-2 tbsp. sugar

1 tsp. Creole seasoning
4 cups shredded cabbage (or 1 large
   bag slaw mix)
1 Red Delicious apple, cored and diced*
½ lb. leftover boiled shrimp, peeled**
Cajun seasoning or salt and pepper,
   to taste

In a large skillet that has a lid, over medium heat, add olive oil. Sauté onion and sausage for 3 minutes.

In a mixing bowl, combine vinegar, beer, sugar depending on desired sweetness, and Creole seasoning. Add to skillet. Raise heat to medium high and bring mixture to a boil.

Stir in cabbage and apple. Reduce heat to medium. Cover and cook for 5 minutes. Remove from heat.

Top with cold leftover boiled shrimp. Serve as a salad or wrap or in a pita pocket.

Serves 4-6 as a side dish

*Use the apple core in a morning smoothie.

**If you prefer warm shrimp, add to cabbage mixture and sauté over medium heat for 1-2 minutes just before serving.

TO COOK IS TO CREATE: What else goes into your boiling pot? Eggs? Chop boiled eggs and add along with leftover shrimp. Brussels sprouts or carrots? Slice and add with the cabbage. Potatoes? Cube and add with the cabbage. If you prefer more of a crunch, add diced celery or shredded raw carrots. Have leftover crawfish? Use it instead of or in addition to shrimp to make a seafood slaw.

Old-Fashioned Boiled Shrimp Stew

This stew begins the old-fashioned way, using shrimp heads and shells to make a shrimp stock. It truly can become an "anything can go in the pot" stew. Want to enjoy it the way I grew up eating it? Top a bowl with a sliced hard-boiled egg.

1 lb. leftover boiled large head-on shrimp
1 tbsp. olive oil
Water to cover
2 bay leaves, divided
12 oz. tasso or smoked sausage, diced
2 tbsp. flour
1 large onion, chopped
2 cloves garlic, minced
1 green bell pepper, chopped
2 celery stalks, chopped
2 cans (14.5 oz. each) stewed tomatoes
2 large Idaho potatoes, cubed
12-oz. bag frozen corn
12-oz. bag frozen cut okra
Louisiana hot sauce, to taste
Creole seasoning, to taste

Peel the shrimp, reserving the shells and heads. Place shrimp in refrigerator.

In a stockpot, over medium-high heat, add oil, shells, and heads. Sauté for 2 minutes.

Cover with water. Add 1 bay leaf. Bring to a boil.

Skim off any foam that rises to the surface. Reduce heat to low and simmer for 15 minutes. Using a fine-mesh strainer, strain stock over a bowl.

In the stockpot, over medium heat, brown the tasso or sausage. Add the flour, stirring until light brown. Add the onions, garlic, pepper, and celery. Continue to cook for 5 minutes.

Add the stewed tomatoes, remaining bay leaf, and shrimp stock. Bring to a boil. Reduce heat to low. Simmer for 30 minutes.

Add potatoes. Continue to simmer 30 additional minutes. Add the corn and okra. Simmer for 15 minutes, adding the boiled shrimp during the last 5 minutes.

Add hot sauce and Creole seasoning.

Serves 4

Tiny Tidbit: The stew can be served over grits or rice.

Leftover Fried Shrimp Poppers

This recipe was inspired by one of my favorite Super Bowl snacks—cheese-stuffed jalapeno poppers. I figured adding fried shrimp to jalapenos, cream cheese, and cheddar cheese could only make my favorite snack even better. I love these with a dab of chili sauce.

1 cup flour
2 tsp. baking powder
¼ cup vegetable, corn, or canola oil
½ cup cold water
4-oz. pkg. cream cheese, softened
¼ cup grated cheddar cheese

1 tsp. Worcestershire sauce
Olive oil spray or nonstick cooking
   spray
12 fresh jalapeno slices
12 leftover fried shrimp, tails
   removed

Preheat oven to 475 degrees.

In a mixing bowl, sift flour and baking powder together. Stir in oil. Slowly stir in the water until mixture resembles a thick pancake batter. Set aside for 15 minutes.

In another bowl, blend cheeses and Worcestershire sauce.

Spray 12 wells of a mini muffin tin with olive oil or nonstick spray. Add 1 tbsp. batter to each well. Top each with 1 tsp. cheese mixture, 1 jalapeno slice, and 1 fried shrimp. Gently press down to cover cheese.

Bake for 12-15 minutes.

TO COOK IS TO CREATE: No leftover fried shrimp? Use leftover chicken nuggets. Don't like it spicy? Substitute pickle slices or pickled okra for the jalapenos.

SWEET AND SOUR FRIED SHRIMP

I never mind eating cold leftover fried shrimp, whether tossed straight into my mouth, onto a salad, or into this sweet and sour sauce (which is almost as quick). I simply stir the shrimp into this tangy, warm, pineapple sauce studded with green peppers. This is not a bright-red sweet and sour sauce, but if you close your eyes, you will never know because the flavors are about the same. I love this dish as an appetizer served over a bed of coleslaw mix or as a meal for two served over rice. It also works well with leftover popcorn shrimp or chicken. Sometimes if using leftover popcorn chicken, I like to add crushed peanuts.

8-oz. can pineapple chunks in own juice
1 tbsp. lemon juice
1 tbsp. light brown sugar, packed
1 tsp. cornstarch
1 tsp. reduced-sodium soy sauce

$^1\!/_4$ tsp. ground ginger
1 tsp. toasted sesame seeds
1 small green bell pepper, diced
Leftover fried shrimp (6-10, depending on size)

In a medium saucepan, over medium-high heat, combine pineapple chunks and juice, lemon juice, brown sugar, cornstarch, soy sauce, ginger, sesame seeds, and bell pepper. Stir continuously until thickened, about 5 minutes. Remove from heat.

Add fried shrimp to the sauce and gently toss. Serve and enjoy.

Tiny Tidbit: Have leftover hushpuppies? Crumble over sautéed green beans for a "Southern" flavor.

Fried Oyster Stuffed Artichokes

I love artichokes, especially stuffed. Leftover fried oysters make an easy stuffing, as their breading works just like breadcrumbs. I like to add the shredded Parmesan cheese before baking because I love brown bits of cheese. If you don't care for it, wait to add until after baking.

1 can artichoke hearts, drained*
    (5-7 count)
4 oz. cream cheese
¼ cup mayonnaise
¼ cup grated Parmesan cheese
¼ tsp. Louisiana hot sauce, or more
    to taste

½ tsp. Worcestershire sauce
½ cup leftover fried oysters
Shredded Parmesan cheese, for
    topping

Cut artichoke hearts in half lengthwise. Place cut side down on paper towels to drain for 5 minutes.

In a mixing bowl, using a rubber spatula, stir cream cheese, mayonnaise, Parmesan cheese, hot sauce, and Worcestershire sauce until well combined. Mince fried oysters (about 4 large or 6 small) in a food processor, and fold into cheese mixture.

Turn over artichoke hearts. Fill each artichoke-heart half with 1 tbsp. mixture, pressing down gently so halves will sit flat.

Preheat oven to 350 degrees.

Place stuffed artichokes on a lightly greased baking sheet and bake for 20-25 minutes or until golden brown.

Top with shredded Parmesan cheese.

*Use liquid to flavor hummus.

TO COOK IS TO CREATE: No artichokes? Use mushrooms instead. No leftover fried oysters? Substitute leftover fried shrimp or even the stuffing from a leftover stuffed crab. If you want to make a dip from this recipe, pull the artichoke hearts apart and line them into the bottom of a small casserole dish. Top with the cheese mixture, then the minced fried oysters. Bake at 350 degrees for 20 minutes. Serve with crackers.

Pickled Fried Catfish

When I was a child, Sunday-afternoon drives became a mission to seek out the best fried catfish and return home "fuller than a tick." These Sunday road trips with my family created many memories beyond the catfish. There were no distractions of electronic devices such as cellphones or the Internet, just family fun . . . and some very serious games of car bingo. I love a cold leftover fried catfish sandwich with coleslaw, but if I don't have slaw, I make this easy recipe instead: simply toss and chill. It looks great on a charcuterie board and can also be added to lettuce for an instant salad.

1¹⁄₂ tbsp. lemon juice
3 tbsp. olive oil
1 tsp. canola oil
1 tsp. dried dill, or 1 tbsp. fresh
1 tsp. dried parsley, or 1 tbsp. fresh

1 leftover fried catfish fillet
1 small red onion, thinly sliced
2 queen olives, minced
Salt and pepper, to taste

Mix lemon juice, oils, and herbs.

Cut leftover fried catfish into 1-in. pieces. In a glass bowl, combine catfish, onions, olives, salt, and pepper.

Pour lemon mixture over catfish. Cover and chill for at least 8 hours or overnight.

Enjoy with crackers, toast, or sliced avocado.

Serves 2 as an appetizer

TO COOK IS TO CREATE: No leftover fried catfish? Use any leftover fried fish or fried shrimp. No queen olives? Add black olives or capers. If you're a garlic lover, mix in a minced clove of garlic. No red onion? Use another onion, including green or shallots. Like it spicy? Add a diced jalapeno or serrano pepper. Toss in minced celery for more crunch. And if you love sundried tomatoes, mince a few and add.

Leftover Fried Seafood Piquant

If you love seafood Creole, you'll love this piquant, or spicy version. This is an easy way to enjoy fried seafood leftovers using common items from the pantry.

4 tbsp. unsalted butter
1 medium onion, chopped
1 green bell pepper, chopped
1 clove garlic, minced
2 green onions, chopped
10-oz. can diced tomatoes and green chilies
8-oz. can tomato sauce

2 dashes Louisiana hot sauce, or to taste
1 bay leaf
1 tsp. Creole seasoning
2 tbsp. water
¾-1 cup leftover fried seafood (shrimp, oysters, and/or catfish)
Cooked rice

In saucepan, over medium heat, melt butter. Sauté onion, pepper, and garlic for 5 minutes.

Add green onions, tomatoes, tomato sauce, hot sauce, bay leaf, seasoning, and water. Stir. Reduce heat to low. Cover and simmer for 30 minutes.

Gently stir in leftover fried seafood. If using leftover fried catfish, cut into pieces before adding. Simmer 5 additional minutes or until seafood is warmed.

Serve over rice.

Serves 2

Tiny Tidbit: This works well with leftover boiled shrimp, too.

Fried Onion Ring Butter

I love onion rings and I love, love this butter. It not only can turn a plain hamburger bun into a mouthwatering one, but it also makes a flavorful topping for a steak. It is a simple blended butter, but feel free to add garlic and fresh herbs, too.

Leftover fried onion rings   **Unsalted butter, softened**

Place cold onion rings in a mini food processor. Pulse until minced.

Add 2 tbsp. butter per ¼ cup onion, and process until fully incorporated.

Spread mixture onto baked rolls, bread, or buns, and bake at 350 degrees for 5 minutes.

TO COOK IS TO CREATE: Have frozen buttered garlic bread or breadsticks? Simply omit the butter from this recipe, sprinkle on minced fried onion rings, and bake according to package directions.

Tiny Tidbit: Don't forget to try this fried onion ring butter on a steak, too!

Cheese Fry Wafers

This recipe came out of my love of cheese fries. Yes, I could have just added cheese to cold French fries and broiled them into a dreamy cheesy combination, but then I would have eaten the whole thing in one sitting. Making cheese fry wafers allows me to satisfy my cheese fry craving a few times and share them with my hubby, who would never eat a cheese fry but loves these. They are just like cheese straws, only made with minced French fries mixed into a dough with butter, flour, and cheese.

1 cup flour
2 tsp. dry mustard
1/4 tsp. cayenne pepper, or to taste
1/2 tsp. Creole seasoning
Pinch of salt
4 tbsp. butter

1/2 cup minced leftover French fries
1 cup grated cheddar cheese
1 egg, beaten
Nonstick cooking spray
Grated Parmesan cheese, for
    topping (optional)

Preheat oven to 400 degrees.

In a bowl, add flour, mustard, cayenne, Creole seasoning, and salt. Use fingers or pastry blender to rub butter into flour until mixture forms fine crumbles.

Mix in French fries, cheddar cheese, and egg. Stir until well combined and mixture begins to stick together. Turn mixture onto lightly floured board.

Knead gently until dough is smooth. Form into a disc and wrap in plastic. Chill for 30 minutes.

Grease a baking sheet with nonstick spray.

Roll teaspoons of dough into small balls. Place balls on baking sheet and gently flatten. (Dough also can be rolled into a log and sliced thinly.)

Sprinkle tops with grated Parmesan cheese, if desired. Bake for 15 minutes.

Makes 24 wafers

Tiny Tidbit: You can also make "breadcrumbs" with leftover fries. Process them into crumbs and spread onto a parchment-lined baking sheet. Spray with olive oil. Bake at 350 degrees for 15 minutes. Use these crispy fry bits to add crunch to steamed vegetables or as a substitute topping on your favorite casserole.

Oven Fried French Fry Fish

I like serving these oven fried fish fillets with malt vinegar for an easy all-in-one fish and chips meal.

2 cups leftover French fries
2 tbsp. grated Parmesan cheese
1 tsp. garlic powder
4 fillets (1 ½ lb. total) catfish,
    trout, or flounder

1 tsp. lemon pepper
2 tbsp. mayonnaise
2 tbsp. Panko breadcrumbs
Olive oil spray
Lemon for serving

Preheat oven to 375 degrees.

Place leftover fries, Parmesan cheese, and garlic powder in a food processor. Pulse until minced.

Rinse fillets and pat dry. Place on a parchment-lined baking sheet.

Mix lemon pepper and mayonnaise together. Spread onto each fish fillet.

Top each fillet with a mound of fry mixture, gently pressing into fish. Sprinkle with Panko breadcrumbs and spray with olive oil.

Bake for 20 minutes or until fish easily flakes with a fork. Squeeze with lemon before serving.

Serves 4

EASY GERMAN-STYLE POTATO PANCAKE

This recipe is so simple, I almost did not include it. But this dish actually inspired my Makeover My Leftover blog. It was the basic recipe I used to jot down on to-go boxes to encourage restaurant customers to take home their leftover fries for a meal the next day.

1 cup leftover French fries
1 egg, beaten
1 tbsp. shredded cheese
1 tsp. favorite seasoning (I love
  garlic powder)

1 tbsp. minced onion
1 1/2 tsp. olive oil
Toppings of choice

Using the large holes of a box grater, grate leftover French fries.

Stir beaten egg into potatoes. Mix in cheese, seasoning, and onion.

In a small cast-iron skillet, over medium heat, heat olive oil until shimmering. Spoon mixture into skillet and press into a pancake. Cook until crispy around edges, about 2 minutes per side.

Invert onto a plate. Top with desired toppings.

Makes 1 pancake

Tiny Tidbit: Make it a meal by topping with a sunny-side-up egg for breakfast, sour cream and chives for lunch, or chili and cheese for dinner!

It's a Southern Thing

Grits, Beans, Rice

GRITS

Did you know there is a "Grits Belt"? No, not one you need to loosen after eating too much grits. The Grits Belt stretches from Texas to Virginia, since that is the area where the majority of grits is sold. I think I'm responsible for getting Louisiana at least one notch in that belt!

I love grits—plain and simple grits with just a touch of butter. I ate grits for breakfast practically every morning when I was a child. I certainly don't have it that often nowadays, but when I do, it is still a comforting way to begin my day. To me, grits is especially nice in a big mug on a cold winter day. The only thing I love more than grits is . . . leftover grits. It is a blank canvas that can absorb so many different flavors.

Leftover Grits Golden Bread

Imagine all the goodness of buttery grits and all the yumminess of golden cornbread . . . together! What could be more Southern? It is similar to hot water cornbread. The hardest part of making this bread is waiting for it to bake. This treat is so easy—no kneading and no rising and only six ingredients. This bread makes a hearty French toast, my favorite way to enjoy it!

$\frac{1}{2}$ cup leftover grits
1 egg, beaten
1 tsp. salt

1 cup cornmeal
2-2$\frac{1}{2}$ cups boiling water
1 tbsp. butter

Preheat oven to 350 degrees.

In a large bowl, mix grits, egg, salt, and cornmeal together. Carefully and slowly stir in boiling water, a little at a time. Continue to add water until a very thin batter is formed.

Heat butter in a loaf pan until melted. Pour batter into hot pan.

Bake for 50-60 minutes or until top is golden brown and cake tester or toothpick inserted comes out clean. Refrigerate leftovers.

Makes 1 loaf

TO COOK IS TO CREATE: I like to keep this bread simple, but think about how many things you could add to the batter to make it a sweet or savory treat. For instance, try using bacon fat in place of the butter or adding crumbled cooked bacon, raisins or dried cranberries, nuts, or fresh herbs.

Tiny Tidbit: Whisk leftover shrimp and grits, crawfish jalapeno grits, or cheese grits into your favorite cornbread batter. Bake as usual.

GRITS AND GRILLADES MEATLOAF

Grillades, for those of you who don't have the privilege of indulging in them just about any day of the week at local restaurants, are pronounced "gree-ahds." They are a Creole dish of meat—veal, pork, beef, or just about anything hunted in Louisiana—browned then braised in a stock with tomatoes (although optional), thyme, bay leaves, and the holy trinity of Creole cooking (bell pepper, onion, and celery). But as with most Louisiana cuisine, you guessed it, anything goes. Most menus serve the grillades over grits. Leftover grits can also be used in meatloaf as an extender for ground beef or used as a filling for this "grillades" meatloaf. For this recipe, I use lean ground beef to balance the fat in the sausage. I do not add any breadcrumbs or egg, just the layers of leftover grits. If you have a favorite meatloaf recipe, use it here. I like to serve this meatloaf with biscuits for mopping up the sauce.

2 links sausage (12 oz. total), casings removed
1 tbsp. olive oil
1 onion, chopped
1 green pepper, chopped
2 cloves garlic, minced
2 celery stalks, diced
1 lb. lean ground beef
14.5-oz. can diced tomatoes, drained, juice reserved

1 cup leftover grits, divided
1 tbsp. red wine vinegar
8 oz. sliced fresh mushrooms
1 tbsp. unsalted butter
1 tbsp. flour
1 cup beef broth
1/4 tsp. thyme
1 bay leaf
Creole seasoning, to taste

Preheat oven to 350 degrees. Grease a meatloaf pan and set aside.

In a food processor, grind sausage. Transfer to a large mixing bowl.

In a skillet, over medium heat, add olive oil and sauté onions for 5 minutes. Add green pepper, garlic, and celery. Sauté for 10 minutes. Set aside to cool for 5 minutes.

To the sausage, add the ground beef, drained tomatoes, and half of the sautéed vegetable mixture. Mix all ingredients by hand. Divide meat mixture into 3 equal parts.

Press 1 layer of meat mixture into bottom of meatloaf pan. Top with 1/2 cup leftover grits, leaving room along edges and ends. Repeat with another meat layer, remaining grits, and last meat layer.

Press down to seal layers. Brush top with red wine vinegar.

Bake covered for 1 hour. Drain. Bake uncovered an additional 15 minutes. Drain, if needed.

To make the sauce, return skillet with sautéed vegetables to medium heat. Add mushrooms and sauté for 5 minutes. Add butter. Stir until melted.

Add flour. Stir constantly for 5 minutes. Add beef broth, reserved tomato juice, thyme, bay leaf, and Creole seasoning. Simmer for 10-15 minutes or until reduced and thickened.

Remove bay leaf. Pour sauce over meatloaf. Return meatloaf to oven, and bake uncovered an additional 5 minutes.

Cover and let sit at least 10 minutes before slicing.

Serves 4

TO COOK IS TO CREATE: What other sautéed veggies may be good? Okra? Zucchini? Try using leftover cheese grits. No leftover grits? Use leftover rice or polenta instead. Want to enjoy the meatloaf for brunch? Serve a slice open face on a biscuit or English muffin, and top with an over-easy egg. Not a meatloaf fan? Make hamburger patties or meatballs stuffed with grits, cook, then top with sauce (no need to drain tomatoes; just add to sauce with the juice). Meatballs are delicious served open face on French bread, topped with Swiss cheese, and broiled until cheese is melted—knife and fork required! The same can be done with any leftover meatloaf slices on toast.

GRITS CHIPS

If you like pork rinds, you'll love these grits chips. This simple recipe may take a bit of time slowly drying in a low-degree oven, but the result is a light, airy, popped chip. After the chips are baked, it's fun to watch them "pop" in the oil and even more fun popping them into your mouth.

½ cup leftover grits   **Creole seasoning**
Oil for frying

Preheat oven to 200 degrees.

Drop grits by teaspoons onto a parchment-lined baking sheet. Gently flatten with a spatula.

Bake for 80 minutes, flipping chips every 20 minutes.

In a heavy-bottomed pot or deep fryer, heat oil to 350 degrees. Fry chips for 30 seconds. Season with Creole seasoning.

Makes 20 chips

RED AND WHITE BEANS

I love red beans and rice. In fact, when asked what I would have if I knew it was my last meal, I always answer red beans and rice. Well, that's part of my answer, as in a part of a seven-course meal! Living in Louisiana offers many opportunities to eat red beans and rice, and I never tire of them. When I see this dish on a menu, I am always tempted to order it, even as a side or just for the leftovers.

As much as I love red beans, white beans also have a special place in my heart and had a place within my MeMaw's, too. It seemed there was always a bowl, the same bowl, of beans hanging out in her fridge. Yes, she had a designated white-bean bowl. I can still see the delicate blue, faded-stitch pattern wrapping around the bowl. That bowl got a lot of use!

Mom and me bellying up to plates of MeMaw's white beans. Look how happy I am!

"Olive" Red Bean Relish

Just like leftover red beans, this dip gets better with time. I like to plan ahead and chill it overnight before enjoying. The flavors may sound crazy, but this dip is always a hit at parties. If serving with chips, I recommend corn tortilla.

2 tbsp. red wine vinegar
1 small red onion, diced
2 tbsp. canola or olive oil
1 cup leftover red beans
1/3 cup chopped pimento-stuffed
   olives

3/4 tsp. sugar
Louisiana hot sauce, to taste
Green onions, diced, for topping
   (optional)
Chips, sliced cooked sausage, or
   boiled shrimp, for dipping

Pour vinegar over diced red onion. Let sit for 10 minutes. Whisk in the oil.

Dice any large pieces of meat in the red beans. Mix red beans and meat thoroughly with olives, sugar, and hot sauce. Cover. Chill for at least 1 hour or overnight.

Garnish with green onions, if using. Serve chilled with chips, cooked sausage, or boiled shrimp.

Makes 1 1/2 cups

Red Beans and Rice Chicken Nachos

Have you ever noticed how many restaurants serve fried chicken along with red beans and rice? They go together like chicken and waffles. This is my way of enjoying and sharing that wonderful combination of flavors in one bite.

6 oz. boneless, skinless chicken
   breast
1 cup self-rising flour
1 1/2 tsp. Creole seasoning
1/4 cup Louisiana hot sauce

Canola oil for frying
1/2 cup leftover red beans
1/4 cup leftover rice
1 green onion, sliced, for topping

Freeze chicken for 1 hour. Then remove chicken and cut into thin slices or "chips."

Mix flour and Creole seasoning together in a bowl. Add hot sauce to another bowl.

Place chicken chips in bowl with hot sauce. Coat well.

Dredge chicken chips in flour.

In a cast-iron pot or deep fryer, heat oil to 375 degrees. Fry chicken chips for 1 minute per side or until golden brown. Remove to paper towels to drain.

In a saucepan, over medium heat, stir red beans and rice together until heated through.

To serve, spoon red beans and rice over fried chicken chips. Garnish with green onions.

Serves 4 as an appetizer

Red Beans and Rice Cornbread Pancakes

Red beans and rice are always better the second time around. I love them so much I even have the leftovers for breakfast at times. Yes, I did say for breakfast, but they also make an inexpensive appetizer for a brunch party. This recipe is very versatile and can also be prepared in a waffle iron for a great waffle.

1 link andouille sausage, cubed
8.5-oz. box cornbread mix
1 cup leftover red beans
1/2 cup leftover rice

1 tsp. vanilla
Powdered sugar and/or maple syrup,
   for topping

Place andouille sausage in a food processor. Mince. In a skillet, over medium heat, cook, stirring constantly, until crispy, about 5 minutes. Set aside.

Prepare cornbread batter according to package instructions (which might require adding an egg and milk). Add the beans, rice, and vanilla. Mix well. Let sit for 10 minutes.

In a nonstick skillet or griddle, over medium heat, drop batter by tablespoons. When first side is full of bubbles, about 1 minute, flip. Cook an additional 1 minute.

Serve red beans and rice cornbread pancakes with crumbled andouille. Top with powdered sugar and/or maple syrup.

Makes 2 1/2 dozen

TO COOK IS TO CREATE: Want to omit the andouille? Substitute bacon. Want to make it sweeter? Add 1 tsp. cinnamon and 1 tbsp. maple syrup along with the vanilla. To make a savory side dish instead, omit the vanilla, and add diced green onions and hot sauce to the batter.

Leftover Red Bean Chili Con Carne

I like to serve this hearty chili over a baked potato with cheese and jalapenos, but it also makes the perfect Frito pie. In this chili con carne, or "chili with meat," I add leftover red beans, which is sure to fuel a bean or no bean debate in some parts, but it enables this chili to be done quickly. My red beans usually contain sausage, and with the combination of ground beef and tomatoes, you can stand a spoon up in this chili. It freezes well, too.

1 lb. lean ground beef
1 large yellow onion, chopped
1 clove garlic, minced
$1/4$ tsp. cumin seed
2 tsp. chili powder
8 oz. beef broth

14.5-oz. can fire-roasted chopped
  tomatoes
1 cup leftover red beans
Pickled jalapeno slices and shredded
  cheddar cheese, for topping
  (optional)

In a Dutch oven, over medium heat, add beef and onion. Cook beef until no longer pink, about 8 minutes. Drain.

Return Dutch oven to stove, and add garlic, cumin, and chili powder. Stir for 1 minute to toast spices. Add broth and tomatoes. Bring to a boil.

Reduce heat to low. Cover and cook for 20 minutes.

Stir in the leftover red beans. Cover and cook an additional 10 minutes, stirring occasionally.

Spoon into serving bowls and top with jalapeno slices and cheese, if desired.

Serves 4

Coconut Curry Red Beans over Cashew Rice Cakes

Coconut Curry Red Beans . . . imagine the classic Louisiana Monday dish on vacation in the Caribbean. Leftover red beans are flavored with sweet potatoes, coconut milk, cumin, curry powder, cayenne pepper, and diced green chiles. No matter what meat I may or may not have in my red beans, I always add a chopped link of andouille or smoked sausage. But it can be omitted. The cashew rice cakes were inspired by the fact that I love cashews in curries. If you happen to have any leftover cashew rice cakes, you must try them for breakfast topped with an over-easy egg!

1 tsp. olive oil
1 onion, chopped
1 link andouille or smoked sausage, chopped
4-oz. can diced green chiles or 1 Anaheim chili, seeded and chopped
1 medium sweet potato, cubed
$1/2$ tsp. cumin seed
1-$1^{1}/2$ tbsp. curry powder

$1/2$ tsp. cayenne pepper
1 cup leftover red beans
$1/2$ cup coconut milk
1 egg, beaten
1 cup leftover rice, preferably jasmine
$1/2$ cup raw cashews, ground
$1/2$ tsp. garam masala*
Coconut flakes and/or raisins, for topping

In a large skillet, over medium heat, add olive oil and sauté onion, sausage, chiles, and sweet potatoes for 5 minutes.

Add cumin, curry powder, and cayenne pepper. Stir for 1 minute to toast seasonings.

Stir in leftover red beans and coconut milk. Reduce heat to low. Simmer for 10-15 minutes.

To make the rice cakes, in a bowl, whisk together egg, rice, cashews, and garam masala. Let mixture sit for 5 minutes.

Drop by $1/4$ cup onto a greased hot griddle, and gently flatten with spatula. Cook 3-4 minutes on each side until brown.

Scoop red bean curry over rice cakes. Sprinkle with coconut flakes and/or raisins.

Serves 4

*If you do not have garam masala, no need to buy any for this little amount. Make a small batch by mixing 2 tsp. ground cumin, 1 tsp. ground cardamom, 1 tsp. black pepper, and ½ tsp. each ground cloves, cinnamon, and nutmeg. Store in an airtight container.

TO COOK IS TO CREATE: No leftover red beans? Use a 16-oz. can creamy-style red kidney beans. Like tomatoes in a curry? Add chopped tomatoes, salsa, or even some bottled chili sauce. Think about what else you enjoy in a curry and try it. No curry powder? Substitute chili powder and paprika. If you want a boost of flavor, drizzle with a spicy mayo. Not in the mood for rice? Omit sweet potatoes from the recipe and serve curry in a baked sweet potato topped with roasted cashews and toasted coconut flakes.

Serving up a taste of the Caribbean with a plateful of Coconut Curry Red Beans Over Cashew Rice Cakes. (Photograph by Minh Kiet)

SPICY AND STEAMY RED BEAN BUNS

Steamed buns filled with a sweet red bean paste are a popular Chinese dessert. Since I am more of a savory than a sweet person, I use leftover red beans with chipotle peppers in adobo sauce to make a spicy paste. The addition of fresh carrots, cilantro, and canned bean sprouts helps balance the heat, but if your spice meter is low, simply cut back on the adobo sauce. Refrigerated canned biscuits make these steamy, pillowy-soft buns a breeze.

7-oz. can chipotle peppers in adobo sauce*

1 clove garlic, peeled

½ cup leftover red beans

1 tube (10-count) refrigerated biscuits, regular sized not flaky

1 large carrot, shredded

14-oz. can bean sprouts, drained**

1 bunch cilantro***

Place 1 chipotle pepper, ½ tsp. adobo sauce, garlic, and leftover red beans in a food processor. Blend into a paste, stopping to scrape down the sides.

Roll out each biscuit into a 3-in. diameter. Add 1 tsp. red bean paste to center of each rolled-out biscuit. Top with 1 tsp. each carrots and bean sprouts.

Rinse cilantro, pat dry, and chop leaves and stems. Top each biscuit with ½ tsp. cilantro and ¼ tsp. adobo sauce. Pull up a side of each biscuit and begin to pinch all the edges together, making pleats around the biscuit to form a tightly sealed "bun."

Using a bamboo steamer over a wok or skillet, or a pot fitted with a steaming basket, add water to bottom of wok or pot and bring to a boil. To prevent sticking, place a silicone liner or parchment paper onto steamer bed. Put "buns" on top. Cover.

Steam for 10 minutes. Turn off heat. Let sit for 5 minutes.

Buns can be dotted with adobo sauce and topped with cilantro, if desired.

Makes 10 buns

*Puree any remaining peppers and sauce. Freeze in ice-cube trays for a quick addition to sauces or soups.

**Use any leftover bean sprouts for a stir-fry.

***Any remaining dried, chopped cilantro leaves and stems can be frozen in small portions in airtight containers. Use as needed when cooking.

Tiny Tidbit: Use this method of steaming filled biscuits for a variety of leftovers. In the summer, I like to use leftover barbeque pulled pork with coleslaw and red onions.

Notes:

_____

_____

_____

_____

_____

_____

_____

Leftover White Bean Shrimp Salad

No matter how you make your white beans, they can be used in this salad (even canned beans in a pinch). This dish is a great reason to pull a container of white beans from the freezer in the summer. It is perfect for stuffing fresh tomatoes, which MeMaw always did with the freshly picked tomatoes from her garden. If I don't have fresh tomatoes, I stuff an avocado or simply stuff this between two slices of bread.

1 clove garlic, minced
3 tbsp. red onion, minced
$1/4$ tsp. white pepper
Pinch of salt
1 tbsp. white wine vinegar
3 tbsp. olive oil
4 large tomatoes

$1^1/2$ cups leftover white beans
$1/2$ lb. cold boiled shrimp, peeled
1 celery stalk, diced
2 green onions, minced
Fresh parsley, chopped (optional)
Lettuce for serving

In a small glass bowl, mix the garlic, red onion, white pepper, salt, and vinegar. Slowly whisk in the olive oil. Let sit for 30 minutes.

Core tomatoes. Cut a thin slice off each top, and if tomatoes do not sit flat, cut a thin slice off each bottom. Using a small spoon, hollow out inside of tomatoes, saving all pulp. Chop pulp and slices, and add to a salad bowl.

Place cored tomatoes face down in a storage container, and chill.

To the salad bowl, add the beans, shrimp, and celery. Stir in the dressing. Mix well.

Set the salad in the refrigerator and let sit for 2 hours or overnight.

Add any tomato juice from storage container, along with green onions, to salad mixture. Stuff each tomato with mixture. Garnish with parsley, if desired. Enjoy over bed of lettuce.

Serves 4

TO COOK IS TO CREATE: Do your white beans contain ham or sausage? If not, add some to this salad, or use crumbled cooked bacon. If you enjoy chopped hard-boiled eggs or diced bell pepper in a potato salad, add some. You can use leftover crawfish tails instead of shrimp.

Nutty Beans and Greens

Use your last cup of white beans to make a hearty meal for one. A side of cornbread makes a tasty addition. If you prefer, you may serve it as a side dish for two, along with baked fish or chicken. If I'm lucky enough to have any leftover boiled shrimp, I add them with the bacon. White beans and greens are always together on our plates, and the pecans provide an unexpected meatiness and crunch.

2 thick slices bacon, roughly chopped
1 shallot, diced
1 red bell pepper, diced
1 clove garlic, minced
2 cups shredded, packed collard or
   mustard greens*

1/2 cup chicken stock
1 cup leftover white beans
1/4 cup chopped pecans
Salt and freshly ground pepper
Louisiana hot sauce, to taste

In a cast-iron skillet that has a lid, over medium heat, cook bacon until crisp, about 6-8 minutes. Remove bacon and set aside, leaving bacon fat in skillet.

Add shallot and red pepper. Cook for 2 minutes. Add garlic and greens. Stir for 1 minute.

Pour the chicken stock over the greens. Cover. Cook for 5 minutes.

Reduce heat to low and add leftover white beans. Cook for 4 minutes. Stir in pecans and let cook an additional 1 minute.

Add salt, pepper, and hot sauce. Top with chopped bacon.

Serves 1 as a meal

*I like to rinse greens in a bowl of water and use a salad spinner to dry. Then I can use the water on my plants. If not using the stems, I chop and freeze them for stir-fries.

Tiny Tidbit: Warm leftover white beans, and serve on a bed of cold kale with flaked tuna and a squeeze of lemon.

CAJUN ANDOUILLE AND OKRA CHILI

I call this a tantalizing marriage of chili and gumbo. It has all the goodness of a gumbo (a roux base, okra, and andouille) and a chili (tomatoes, beans, and spices). I got the idea while developing a recipe for a major brand. It wasn't going in the direction I had planned, but the concept for this chili was born. The next time I had leftover white beans, I tried it and served it. I knew it was a success when my hubby said the next time he went to the duck camp, he wanted to bring this chili to share with the guys. In camp language, that is a huge compliment! If you don't have any leftover white beans, canned beans may be used.

2 tbsp. canola oil
2 tbsp. all-purpose flour
4 celery stalks, chopped
1 green pepper, chopped
1 onion, chopped
2 cloves garlic, minced
1 lb. andouille or smoked sausage, diced
¼ tsp. cayenne pepper
⅛ tsp. smoked paprika
½ tsp. cumin
2 bay leaves
1-2 tbsp. ancho chili powder
1 cup beef broth or stock
1 tsp. Worcestershire sauce
2 cups leftover white beans
28-oz. can whole Marzano peeled tomatoes
¼ tsp. Louisiana hot sauce
1½ cups frozen cut okra (about 5 oz.)
Banana pepper rings, for topping

In a large cast-iron or enameled cast-iron Dutch oven, over medium heat, combine the oil and flour. Using a wooden spoon, stir slowly and constantly for approximately 6 minutes, to make a roux the color of dark caramel.

Add celery, green pepper, onion, and garlic, and continue to stir for 4-5 minutes, or until wilted. Add the sausage and seasonings—cayenne, paprika, cumin, bay leaves, and chili powder. Continue to stir for 3 minutes.

Add the beef broth slowly until fully incorporated with the roux. Then add Worcestershire sauce, leftover white beans, and can of tomatoes with ½ can water. Raise heat to medium high. Bring mixture to a boil.

Reduce heat to medium low. Add hot sauce. Simmer for 1 hour, stirring occasionally, to break up tomatoes.

Add frozen cut okra. Continue to simmer for 10 minutes. Serve chili topped with banana pepper rings.

Serves 4-6

TO COOK IS TO CREATE: Want to make it vegetarian? Omit the andouille, use vegetable broth instead of beef, and add corn or more okra. Don't like okra? Substitute cubed yellow squash and zucchini, and cook the same way. If you have leftover rotisserie chicken, add it during the last 10 minutes. Spice the chili up as much as you like—add more chili powder, fresh sliced peppers, chipotle pepper with adobo sauce, or more cayenne pepper or hot sauce. Don't have any beef broth or stock on hand? Substitute a dark beer. If you have any leftovers from this dish, make chili mac and cheese or serve over rice.

Notes:

_____

_____

_____

_____

_____

_____

_____

RICE

Rice is a staple in the South and the base for so many traditional dishes. Everything goes with rice—at least in Louisiana. In college, I joked that I could eat rice in the cafeteria for breakfast, lunch, dinner, and any time in between.

I might have gotten "riced" out then but have since found an appreciation not only for perfectly cooked rice but also the many possibilities for using leftover rice. It is so versatile. That is why the South has an unwritten law that rice must always be in the pantry. Rice heated with butter, fresh lemon juice, lemon zest, and Parmesan cheese is an anytime treat of mine.

Rice Rounds

These simple little rounds make serving leftover beans a breeze. Imagine a handheld bite of beans and rice. The rounds can even become what I call "mock" sushi, when topped with boiled shrimp and a dab of cocktail sauce. Add in any seasonings to complement the toppings.

Olive oil spray
1 cup leftover rice

1 tbsp. mayonnaise

Preheat oven to 375 degrees. Spray 18 wells of a mini muffin tin with olive oil.

In a mixing bowl, using a rubber spatula, combine leftover rice and mayonnaise. Let sit for 5 minutes.

Take mixture by tablespoons and, using your hands, roll into balls. Press rice down into wells of mini muffin tin. Form an indentation on top of each rice round.

Bake for 15 minutes.

Run a butter knife around the edges and gently remove each round. Top with desired leftovers.

Italian Rice Rounds

Rice rounds are so versatile they can even make a nice hot "caprese style" appetizer.

Olive oil spray
1 cup leftover rice
1 tbsp. mayonnaise
1 tbsp. grated Parmesan cheese
$\frac{1}{2}$ tsp. Italian seasoning
1 pt. cherry tomatoes, cut in half
   horizontally

8 oz. fresh mozzarella pearls
$\frac{1}{4}$ cup pesto
Balsamic vinegar and shredded
   Parmesan cheese, for topping

Preheat oven to 375 degrees. Spray each well of a mini muffin tin with olive oil.

In a mixing bowl, combine rice, mayonnaise, grated Parmesan cheese, and Italian seasoning. Let sit for 5 minutes.

Take mixture by tablespoons and, using your hands, roll into balls. Press rice down into wells of mini muffin tin. Top each with a tomato half, then a mozzarella pearl, and then another tomato half.

Bake for 15 minutes.

Top each round with pesto. Bake an additional 5 minutes.

Run a butter knife around the edges and gently remove each round. Drizzle with balsamic vinegar and sprinkle with shredded Parmesan cheese.

Grilled Vegetable Rice Salad

This makes a nice summer lunch for two. It's a refreshing way to use up bits of leftover grilled vegetables as well as tomatoes, cucumbers, and other salad fixings.

$\frac{1}{2}$ cup chopped leftover grilled vegetables

$\frac{1}{4}$ cup chopped assorted salad fixings*

1 cup leftover rice

1 tbsp. plus 1 tsp. red wine vinegar

2 tbsp. plus 2 tsp. olive oil

$\frac{1}{4}$ tsp. salt

$\frac{1}{4}$ tsp. pepper

Lettuce or spinach leaves for serving

Mix roughly chopped leftover grilled vegetables and salad fixings with leftover rice.

In a small bowl, whisk together the red wine vinegar, olive oil, salt, and pepper. Pour over rice and vegetable mixture, and toss well.

Divide mixture in half and pack tightly into 2 lightly greased 4-oz. ramekins. Chill for at least 1 hour or overnight.

To remove molded salad, place a salad plate over a ramekin. Invert. Give ramekin a few taps to release salad. Repeat with other salad.

Serve with lettuce or spinach leaves alongside.

Serves 2

*Salad fixings can include any cheese, lunch meat, olives, tomatoes, cucumbers, etc.

Leftover Rice Gone Wild

You will never look at plain white rice the same again! This makes not only a quick side but also a stuffing. I absolutely love it for stuffed squash.

1 tbsp. butter
1 small onion, chopped
1 bell pepper, chopped
8 oz. fresh mushrooms, chopped
2 celery stalks, chopped
1/8 tsp. celery seed

1/8 tsp. ground sage
1/8 tsp. dried thyme
1/8 tsp. dried rosemary
1/2 cup beef broth
1 1/2 cups leftover rice
1/4 cup chopped pecans

In a saucepan, over medium heat, melt butter. Add onion, pepper, mushrooms, celery, celery seed, sage, thyme, and rosemary. Sauté for 10 minutes, stirring often.

Add beef broth, and scrape up any brown bits.

Mix in rice. Cover, and reduce heat to low. Let cook for 5 minutes. Remove from heat.

Add pecans, mixing lightly with a fork. Serve as a side or use as a stuffing.

Makes 2 cups

Tiny Tidbit: Mix softened cream cheese and shredded cheddar into leftover rice, and use to stuff jalapenos.

Southwest Egg and Rice Breakfast Tostada

This recipe was inspired by a great dish I had on a trip out West. When I saw this dish scribbled in the corner of a chalkboard, in a small café in the middle of nowhere, I inquired. I was told it's like huevos rancheros, only different! Since I never met any huevos rancheros I didn't like, I quickly ordered a plate. I was not disappointed. The tostadas were a hearty meal that fortified me for an entire day of hiking. The original dish used the most amazing authentic Southwest rice mixed with tomatoes, corn, peppers, and black beans. My dish uses leftover rice, but the flavors of the creative toppings take me back to that small café.

2 eggs, beaten
$1/2$ cup milk
$1/4$ tsp. chili powder
1 tbsp. grated cheddar cheese
$1/4$ cup leftover rice

3 (6 in.) corn tortillas
$1/2$ cup leftover red beans, mashed,
   or refried beans
Assorted toppings

Mix beaten eggs, milk, and chili powder until well blended. Fold in cheese and rice.

Heat a greased skillet over medium heat. Drop mixture by tablespoons onto skillet (you should have 6 patties). Cook until eggs begin to set. Flip, and cook an additional 1 minute. Remove to a warm plate.

Heat the tortillas one at a time in the skillet. Remove.

Add the beans to the skillet. Stir until hot.

To assemble, spread beans onto tortillas. Top each with 2 egg-and-rice patties.

Makes 3 tostadas

TO COOK IS TO CREATE: Get creative with the toppings. Think grated cheddar cheese, sliced avocado, sliced black olives, diced tomatoes or onions, salsa, guacamole, sour cream, and sliced jalapenos or banana peppers. Have leftover rotisserie chicken? Add it as a topping, too. No refried beans or leftover red beans? Use black beans or leftover chili. In place of corn tortillas, you can use taco shells, flour tortillas, biscuits, or even chips! Have any leftover corn? Add it to the egg and rice mixture.

Coconut Raisin Leftover Rice

Those who know me know I hate raisins, but I love this rice. Why? Hmmmm . . . it just might be that the raisins are soaked in rum. Who am I kidding? There's no "might" about it; that is the sole reason. This recipe combines sweet and savory flavors that pair well with spicy dishes and grilled meats.

2 tbsp. rum	¼ cup shredded coconut
¼ cup raisins	¼ cup firmly packed brown sugar
2 tbsp. butter	¼ tsp. ground ginger
2 cups leftover rice	Squeeze of lime (optional)

Pour the rum over the raisins and let sit.

In a saucepan that has a lid, over medium-low heat, melt the butter. Gently stir in the rice, breaking up any large clumps. Cover. Heat, stirring occasionally, for 5 minutes.

Stir in the raisins, coconut, brown sugar, and ginger. Cook an additional 2 minutes.

Squeeze with lime, if desired. Serve warm.

Makes 2 cups

TO COOK IS TO CREATE: Not a rum fan? Try bourbon. No raisins? Use dried cranberries or another dried fruit. If you don't have shredded coconut, substitute coconut milk for the butter. Want to spice it up more? Try using cinnamon, cardamom, cloves, and curry powder. Want to add a topping? Sprinkle with toasted nuts or toasted coconut flakes. If you're craving something even sweeter, turn this rice dish into a sweet treat by omitting the lime and soaking the raisins in coffee spiked with cordials such as amaretto, Frangelico, or Irish cream.

Picnic in the Park

Comfort Food and Beyond

When I was a child, a picnic in the park meant going to the iconic City Park of New Orleans. This was always a day spent with family. I loved these picnics under the big oak trees of City Park, and so did my mother, aunts, and cousins, who enjoyed them in their own childhoods. Four sculptured lions guard the Peristyle, built in 1907 overlooking a bayou. It was a generational tradition in my family to get a picture taken on one of the beloved lions. These photos would become a record of growth. Forget charts; you were measured by where your feet fell on the side of the lion. These perfect picnic days always ended with a ride on the Carousel or, as we used to say, the "flying horses."

The food would include the standards, such as my MeMaw's potato salad and deviled eggs. You could bet on a jar of pickles making a debut on one end of the table and a watermelon begging to be sliced open on the other end. A bucket of fried chicken was a clear sign that extra family would be joining us. Fresh-squeezed lemonade was the drink of choice. Just thinking of sipping the cold, tart beverage from my small cup makes my lips pucker even now. On cooler picnic days, I was always delighted to see a large plaid thermos pulled out of the picnic basket. No, it wasn't coffee or hot chocolate; it was filled with chili and cooked hot dogs. I always thought of it as a special treat to sit outside in the cool breeze enjoying a chili dog. I would usually wear a drop of chili on my clothes for the rest of the day. These wonderful memories still put a smile on my face.

PIMENTO-CHEESE PASTA

I love macaroni and cheese, and I love the richness that leftover pimento cheese adds to this cream sauce. This cheese sauce is also delicious over steamed vegetables, a baked potato, or a hot dog. At our picnics, my MeMaw's pimento-cheese pecans (see below) always disappeared quickly.

2 tbsp. unsalted butter
2 tbsp. all-purpose flour
1 cup milk or half-and-half
$\frac{1}{4}$ tsp. garlic powder
$\frac{1}{4}$ tsp. paprika

$\frac{1}{4}$ tsp. Louisiana hot sauce
$\frac{1}{2}$ cup leftover pimento cheese
8 oz. shaped pasta
Shredded cheese, for topping
    (optional)

In a medium saucepan, over low heat, melt butter. Whisk in flour. Slowly add milk or half-and-half, garlic powder, paprika, and hot sauce. Whisk until thickened.

Stir in leftover pimento cheese until melted.

Cook pasta according to package directions, but do not drain.* Using a slotted spoon, add pasta to cheese sauce and toss. Top with shredded cheese, if desired.

Serves 2

*Let pasta water cool, portion into ice-cube trays, and freeze. Store frozen cubes in an airtight container, and use to thicken sauces.

Tiny Tidbit: If you still have a bit of leftover pimento cheese, make MeMaw's pimento-cheese pecans! Toast pecan halves, and let cool. Spread pimento cheese on a pecan half, and top with another pecan half. Repeat with remaining pecans.

Old-Fashioned Pickle Juice Cheese Crock

A big jar of pickles was a staple on our picnic table. It was kept open, making it easy to swing in, grab one, and go, usually as my brother and I played a game of tag. The leftover pickle juice in the jar always reappeared in a fried chicken brine or in this cheese crock. I'm lucky to still have the small tan and brown glazed crock with the hinged lid that kept this cheese mixture safely under wraps . . . until my Pawsie and I opened it.

4 oz. cheddar cheese, grated
1 clove garlic, minced
½ tbsp. Worcestershire sauce
¼ tsp. dry mustard

¼ tsp. Louisiana hot sauce
3 oz. leftover pickle juice*
Cajun seasoning, to taste

Blend all ingredients together well. Place in a clean jar or crock, packing down tightly. Close lid.

Store in refrigerator for 2 weeks, or freeze after letting set for 2 days. Serve with grilled sausages, burgers, hot dogs, or warm pretzels.

Makes a 5-oz. crock

*Beer or pickled jalapeno juice can be substituted for pickle juice.

TO COOK IS TO CREATE: Think about all the different kinds of cheese and flavors of beer available. How could changing each change the depth of flavor? I like to add diced jalapenos to my cheese, especially when using the pickled jalapeno juice, for a spicy spread. What other ingredients could you add? Chopped toasted pecans provide a nice texture. How about adding diced pickles, onions, pimentos, or olives? Black olives blend nicely with white cheddar and Emmental cheese. If you don't have pickle juice, pickled jalapeno juice, or beer, try wine.

Tiny Tidbit: If you have a jar with leftover pickle juice, add some to deviled eggs or potato salad. Or place shredded cabbage and carrots in the jar, shake, chill overnight, and use to top sandwiches, hot dogs, or burgers.

SPICY ONION CHEESE CRACKERS

The first time I made these for a party, I was told I should call them "Gone in a Flash Crackers." I always have the ingredients on hand, which means I can quickly bake up a batch. Forget regular cheese crackers. These crackers get their spiciness from hot sauce and Creole seasoning, their crispness from potato chips, and their sharp onion flavor from grated sweet onions. These are perfect for simply snacking, dipping, or topping a soup or salad. They are a must-try on a Caesar salad.

½ stick unsalted butter, softened
½ cup freshly grated cheese
    (cheddar, Colby Jack, or pepper
    Jack)
½ cup all-purpose flour

½ tsp. Louisiana hot sauce
½ tsp. Creole seasoning, divided
½ cup crushed leftover potato chips
½ cup grated onion

Preheat oven to 350 degrees.

Using a wooden spoon, cream butter. Add cheese, flour, hot sauce, and half of the Creole seasoning. Blend lightly. Fold in chips and onion.

Using your hands, take dough by teaspoons and roll into small balls. Place on a parchment-lined baking sheet. Using a fork, gently flatten into crackers.

Bake for 16-18 minutes or until light brown. Sprinkle remaining Creole seasoning over crackers. Let cool and enjoy.

Store in a covered container for up to 1 week.

Makes 30 crackers

Tiny Tidbit: If you have stale chips or cereal, revive them on a baking sheet in a 350-degree oven for 2-3 minutes. Let cool and enjoy!

Refreshing Watermelon Rind Granita

When I was young, there was a house in our neighborhood that sold small cups of frozen flavored ice for a dime. It was always so convenient to ride over on my bike and buy one when the summer heat got to be too much. This granita is a refreshing shaved-ice treat utilizing all the flavor left in the watermelon rind.

Leftover watermelon rind   1 tbsp. fresh lime juice
$\frac{1}{3}$ cup sugar   1$\frac{1}{2}$-2 oz. vodka or gin (optional)*
$\frac{1}{2}$ cup hot water

Using a vegetable peeler, remove a thin layer of the green part of the watermelon rind. Cube remaining rind, about 2 cups. Place in a food processor. Process until minced, resulting in 1 cup.

Stir sugar into water. Keep stirring until all the sugar has dissolved. Stir in the lime juice and watermelon rind.

Transfer the mixture to a shallow glass or ceramic dish. Cover. Freeze for 1 hour.

Using a fork, scrape the ice. Replace cover, and return to freezer.

After 2 hours, use a fork to scrape ice into serving glass.

Serves 4

*To make an adult granita, add vodka or gin along with the lime juice, and increase cubed watermelon rind by $\frac{1}{2}$ cup.

Watermelon Rind French Toast Sticks

Sounds crazy, I know, but this is a unique treat. I hit on the idea one day by thinking that since everything is good fried, why not try watermelon rind? The key to the success of this recipe is the "air dry" time. It helps get the sticks extra crispy on the outside. Prep these for breakfast before going to bed.

Leftover watermelon rind
1 egg
1 tbsp. orange juice
$\frac{1}{2}$ tsp. vanilla
1 cup all-purpose flour

$\frac{1}{2}$ tsp. cinnamon
Oil for frying
Powdered sugar and maple syrup for
   serving

Using a vegetable peeler, remove a thin layer of the green part of the watermelon rind. Slice remaining rind into sticks, about 1 cup. Set sticks on a plate in the refrigerator overnight to "air dry."

In a bowl, whisk egg, orange juice, and vanilla. In another bowl, blend flour and cinnamon. Dip each rind into the egg then flour mixture.

Pan fry in hot oil, for 3 minutes per side. Serve with powdered sugar and maple syrup.

Serves 2

Tiny Tidbit: If you love pepper jelly, summer it up with watermelon. Add diced watermelon rind to a saucepan, cover with water, boil for 5 minutes, and drain. Use in your favorite pepper jelly recipe.

ROASTED WATERMELON RIND AND POTATOES

Roasting watermelon rind with new potatoes adds a depth of texture and flavor. The roasted rind holds up well and brings a lightness to the potatoes. If I do not have any potatoes, I love to roast the rind with cubed carrots. This recipe is simple. It is just equal parts cubed new potatoes and rind tossed with just enough olive oil to lightly coat, seasoned with salt and pepper, and baked. I like to peel a little of the green skin off the rind before roasting, but if you prefer more of an al dente bite, feel free to leave it on.

Leftover watermelon rind, cubed
New potatoes, cubed
Olive oil

Salt and pepper, to taste
Green onions, minced

Preheat oven to 400 degrees.

Toss equal parts cubed rind and potatoes with just enough olive oil to lightly coat. Season with salt and pepper. Spread onto a parchment-lined baking sheet.

Bake for 45 minutes, tossing every 15 minutes.

Stir in green onions and serve.

Tiny Tidbit: Freshen up your favorite store-bought salsa by adding diced watermelon rind.

Hot Honey Fried Chicken Crostini

I love to serve these for a party when I'm looking for a heavier appetizer. They are always a hit. If you have leftover fried chicken and hot honey sauce, you must try it over a waffle or biscuit for breakfast.

1-2 pieces leftover fried chicken, depending on size
1 bay leaf
1 clove garlic
1 tsp. black peppercorns
1 tbsp. butter
1 tbsp. all-purpose flour
$\frac{1}{2}$ tsp. Creole seasoning
$\frac{1}{4}$ cup mayonnaise, divided
1 small French bread, sliced
1 tbsp. honey
1 tsp. Louisiana hot sauce, or to taste
2 green onions, sliced, for topping

Remove skin from chicken. Set aside. Separate meat and bones, and chop meat. Return meat to refrigerator.

In a small stockpot, add chicken bones, bay leaf, garlic, and peppercorns. Cover with water. Bring to a boil. Skim off any foam. Reduce heat to low and simmer 1-1½ hours. Add more water if needed during simmering to yield 1 cup stock. Strain.

In a small saucepan, over medium-low heat, melt butter and slowly whisk in the flour, continuing to whisk until smooth, about 5 minutes. Slowly whisk in the stock until smooth. Add chicken meat and Creole seasoning. Cook for 3-5 minutes into a thick gravy.

Place chicken skin in a food processor. Mince. In a cast-iron skillet, over medium-high heat, fry the minced chicken crumbs, rendering the fat until the crumbs are brown and crisp, like bacon bits.

Using all except for 2 tsp. mayonnaise, spread each bread slice with mayonnaise. Broil for 3-4 minutes until golden brown.

Whisk together honey, hot sauce, and remaining 2 tsp. mayonnaise until smooth.

To assemble, top crostini with chicken gravy, crispy chicken bits, and sliced green onions, then drizzle with hot honey sauce.

Makes 8-10 crostini

Leftover Fried Chicken Okra Ramen

Fried chicken on Mardi Gras Day is a tradition for my family and many others. To me, it would not be Fat Tuesday without a box of spicy fried chicken. After a whole day of revelry, this ramen may not be a cure-all hangover meal, but it certainly helps. I created this recipe by merging the classic Southern dish of okra and tomatoes with an Asian noodle dish featuring onions, green chiles, and spicy red chili paste.

2-3 pieces leftover fried chicken
3 tbsp. olive oil, divided
2 tsp. red chili paste
1/2 lb. fresh okra, washed, dried,
    sliced lengthwise
1 onion, sliced
1 clove garlic, minced
4.5-oz. can diced green chiles
14.5-oz. can diced tomatoes
6 oz. ramen noodles

For the Stock:
1 onion, quartered
2 cloves garlic, cut in half
1 bay leaf

Remove skin from chicken. Set aside. Separate meat and bones. Return meat to refrigerator.

To make the stock, in a small stockpot, add chicken bones, onions, garlic, and bay leaf. Cover with water. Bring to a boil. Skim off any foam. Reduce heat to low, and simmer for 1 to 1 1/2 hours. Add more water if needed during simmering to yield 1 1/2 cups stock. Strain.

Place chicken skin in a food processor. Mince. In a cast-iron skillet, over medium-high heat, fry the minced chicken crumbs, rendering the fat until the crumbs are brown and crisp, like bacon bits. Save for topping.

To the cast-iron skillet, over medium-high heat, add 2 tbsp. olive oil and the chili paste. Add the okra and sauté for 5 minutes. Remove from heat.

In a saucepan, over medium heat, add remaining olive oil. Add sliced onion and minced garlic. Sauté for 5 minutes until softened.

Add diced green chiles and tomatoes. Continue to cook, stirring occasionally, for 10 minutes. Add the chicken, okra, and stock. Bring to a boil.

Add the ramen noodles. Reduce heat to low. Cover and simmer for 5 minutes.

Top the finished ramen with the crispy chicken bits.

Makes 6 cups

TO COOK IS TO CREATE: What kinds of vegetables do you enjoy? Substitute your favorite fresh vegetables for the okra, such as mushrooms. What other proteins could you add? Shrimp? If you enjoy egg in your ramen, add it. Love pad thai? Add crushed peanuts to the crispy chicken bits for the topping. And if you have any leftovers of those crispy chicken bits, use them as you would bacon bits—on salads, soups, baked potatoes, loaded fries, or sautéed green beans.

Notes:

_____

_____

_____

_____

_____

_____

_____

Fried Chicken Chowder

This recipe was inspired by a story shared by a friend. She said that when she was growing up with her five siblings, their mother would always save any bones and add them to a pot of water flavored with broth packets and whatever vegetables were on hand. After hearing that story, I challenged myself to make a pot of chowder using only bones and a few ingredients.

1 leftover fried chicken breast or thigh
$1/2$ cup diced seasoning: celery, onions, garlic, green peppers
1 bay leaf
6 cups water

4.5-oz can diced green chiles
5 small new potatoes, cubed
10 oz. frozen corn
Salt and pepper, to taste
Shredded cheddar cheese for topping

Remove skin from chicken. Set aside. Separate meat and bones. Return meat to refrigerator.

In a medium stockpot, add chicken bones, seasoning, bay leaf, and water. Bring to a boil. Reduce heat to low, and simmer for 1 to $1^1/2$ hours. Add more water if needed. Strain and return chicken broth to stockpot.

Add chiles and potatoes. Simmer until potatoes are tender, 10-12 minutes.

Let mixture cool slightly, then transfer to a blender or use an immersion blender. Blend until smooth. If blender is used, return mixture to stockpot. Turn heat to medium.

Add the chicken, frozen corn, and salt and pepper. Heat for 10 minutes.

Place chicken skin in a food processor. Mince. In a cast-iron skillet, over medium-high heat, fry the minced chicken crumbs, rendering the fat until the crumbs are brown and crisp, like bacon bits. Save for topping.

Top the finished chowder with cheddar cheese and crispy chicken bits.

Serves 4

TO COOK IS TO CREATE: Have a cooked sausage link or chopped ham in the freezer? Add it with the chicken. What other vegetables do you have in the freezer? Mixed vegetables, peas, or lima beans? Add them instead of corn. If you want to spice it up more, use chipotle or jalapeno peppers. Want to turn the chowder into a Mexican fiesta? Season with chili powder and top with dollop of salsa. Want to lighten the chowder? Use cubed sweet potatoes instead of new potatoes. If you enjoy a loaded potato, finish the chowder with a dollop of sour cream and chives. Prefer a thinner chowder? Add cream or milk to desired consistency during the last 2 minutes of cooking.

Notes:

_____

_____

_____

_____

_____

_____

_____

Lemonade Chicken Nuggets

Iced tea and lemonade were the beverages of choice at our picnics. I was never an iced tea fan and am still not to this day, but I love a cold glass of lemonade. A tall glass of lemonade is synonymous with carefree days of summer. There was never a summer day that my mom didn't have a large pitcher of lemonade in the fridge with a stack of cups on the side. I used to dread the day when I would open the fridge and the pitcher would be gone, a sure sign that school was about to begin. Each summer, my mom and I would travel to California to visit her best friend, who is an outstanding cook. Her casual cooking days could be features in a magazine. This recipe is an adaptation of her Chinese-style fried chicken, which she always made for us.

1 cup flour
2 tsp. baking powder
1/4 cup oil (vegetable, corn, or canola)
1/2 cup cold water
1/2 tsp. vanilla
1 lb. boneless, skinless chicken
   breasts, cubed
2 tbsp. leftover lemonade
1 tbsp. low-sodium soy sauce
1/4 tsp. garlic powder
Nonstick cooking or olive oil spray

For the Sauce:
1 cup leftover lemonade
1 tbsp. honey
1/2 tsp. ground ginger
1 tsp. cornstarch

In a mixing bowl, blend flour and baking powder together. Stir in oil, and slowly stir in water until mixture resembles a thick pancake batter. Add vanilla. Set aside.

Preheat oven to 475 degrees.

Place chicken into a bowl. In a small bowl, mix lemonade, soy sauce, and garlic powder together. Pour mixture over chicken. Set aside for 10 minutes.

Spray a mini muffin tin with nonstick cooking or olive oil spray.

Using a toothpick, pick up each cube of chicken and dip it in the batter. Place each cube into a well of the tin. Spray the tops of chicken with nonstick cooking or olive oil spray.

Bake for 16-18 minutes or until a toothpick comes out clean.

Run a butter knife around each well to loosen nuggets before popping out of tin.

To make the lemonade sauce, in a small saucepan, over medium-high heat, add lemonade, honey, ginger, and cornstarch. Mix well. Bring mixture to a boil, whisking occasionally until thickened, about 5 minutes.

Serve the sauce over the chicken nuggets, on the side for dipping, or over leftover fried rice.

Makes 24

TO COOK IS TO CREATE: Instead of vanilla, what other flavor or extracts can be added to the batter? How about a liqueur? If you want more lemon taste, add lemon zest to the batter. What other nuggets can you use besides chicken? Try pork, fish, and vegetables such as yellow squash or zucchini. Do you make any flavored lemonades? Cherry lemonade would result in a tasty sweet and sour sauce here. If you don't like ginger, try Chinese five spice powder. Like it spicy? Add cayenne pepper to the sauce and hot sauce to the chicken!

Notes:

_____

_____

_____

_____

_____

_____

PB & J Chicken Legs

This recipe was created from a story that a friend related to me about her young daughter, who was "stuck" on peanut butter and jelly sandwiches. She would eat one for lunch, and it was all she wanted for dinner. My friend was worried that this "kick" would suddenly stop and she would be looking at two big jars of peanut butter and jelly in her pantry. She asked if I had a more "grownup way" to enjoy PB & J. I kept thinking about the famous meatballs glazed with grape jelly and chili sauce that everyone seems to love . . . except me! Then I thought about how much I like peanut sauce and got this idea. As a child, I used to get on peanut butter and jelly kicks, too. Sometimes my old faithful PB & J sandwich would have to accompany me even on the picnic in the park. I still enjoy one for lunch every now and then with a tall glass of cold milk, but if I want PB & J for dinner, this is it. This recipe is an easy one and you will be surprised by the flavors. The peanut butter helps keep the chicken juicy, and the jelly makes a nice finger-licking glaze.

Nonstick cooking or olive oil spray
$\frac{1}{3}$ cup leftover peanut butter
   (smooth or crunchy)
1 tbsp. olive oil
$\frac{1}{2}$ tsp. cinnamon
$\frac{1}{2}$ tsp. ground ginger

6 chicken legs, skin on (1 $\frac{1}{2}$ lb.)
$\frac{1}{2}$ cup grape jelly
1 tbsp. chicken broth*
Dashes of Louisiana hot sauce
   (optional)

Preheat oven to 450 degrees.

Spray a broiler pan with nonstick cooking or olive oil spray.

In a small bowl, mix peanut butter, olive oil, cinnamon, and ginger together.

Using your fingers, gently loosen the skin around the chicken legs. Pat dry. Stuff the peanut butter mixture under the skin. Make sure to get it completely under the skin, to prevent it from burning.

Place the chicken legs around the pan, with the smaller end of the legs facing inwards.

Bake for 40-45 minutes or until internal temperature is 165 degrees.

In a saucepan, over high heat, bring jelly, chicken broth, and hot sauce (if using) to a boil. Reduce heat to low and simmer 5 minutes, whisking occasionally. Remove from heat. Let cool for 5 minutes.

Brush the grape jelly mixture onto the chicken. Return to the oven. Broil for 3-5 minutes.

*Freeze leftover chicken broth in an ice-cube tray. Remove and store in the freezer in a sealed container for sauce-ready portions.

TO COOK IS TO CREATE: Think about how the taste would change with different jelly or jam flavors. I love orange marmalade with the ginger. How about substituting soy sauce for the olive oil for an Asian flair? What do you like on your PB & J sandwich? You could add any of those flavors to this chicken. If you like it very spicy, replace the olive oil with hot sauce and change the seasoning to cayenne and paprika.

Notes:

_____

_____

_____

_____

_____

_____

_____

_____

Roasted Pepper, Sausage, and Apple Leftover Potato Salad

No one, absolutely no one, made potato salad like my MeMaw, and no picnic was complete without it. I always ate my fair share of this addictive dish served in her blue-rimmed bowl. I'm sure the leftover bacon fat she added was part of the reason. I can still see the can beside her stove that held all the bacon lusciousness. The first time I created this recipe by repurposing potato salad, I was not consciously thinking that the day was the anniversary of my MeMaw's passing. Once I realized that, I could not help but chuckle knowing full well that I would never make over her potato salad. Not only was there no improving it; there were never any leftovers to make over.

1 cup leftover potato salad
1 link smoked sausage, sliced
1 apple, diced*

4 small sweet peppers, sliced, or 1
   large bell pepper, cubed*
1 tsp. garlic powder

Preheat oven to 425 degrees.

In a large bowl, mix all ingredients. Spread mixture onto a parchment-lined baking sheet.

Bake for 45 minutes, tossing and spreading out mixture every 15 minutes.

*Don't forget that the apple core can be used when making tea, and the stems and seeds of the peppers can be used to flavor olive oil.

Makes 2 hearty sides

Tiny Tidbit: To make pimento-cheese potato salad, add pimentos and a combination of shredded sharp cheddar and Monterey Jack to leftover potato salad. This is tasty stuffed in a tomato!

Doubly Devilish Cornbread Muffins

This recipe dates to when I did not fully write out recipes but only offered "suggestions" on how to use leftovers. I almost decided not to include it in this book. However, I love deviled eggs and these cornbread muffins too much. As a child, I would see how many deviled eggs I could stuff in my mouth at once. Now I see how quickly I can stuff the first bite of these muffins in my mouth. Whether the cornbread batter is homemade or from a store-bought mix, the deviled eggs settle in and bake on their cornbread cushion. I love to bite into the muffin to the welcome surprise of a warm deviled egg with the slight sweetness and spiciness of the pepper jelly.

Prepared cornbread batter, divided **Pepper jelly**
Leftover deviled eggs

Pour half of batter into the wells of a nonstick muffin tin, filling halfway. Nestle 1 leftover deviled egg into each well. Top each with $\frac{1}{2}$ tsp. pepper jelly.

Finish pouring batter into wells over eggs.

Bake according to recipe or package directions.

Remove and enjoy right away. Refrigerate any leftovers.

Tiny Tidbit: Still have leftover deviled eggs? Dice and add to cold macaroni and cheese, then use as a stuffing for baked tomatoes or bell peppers.

Tomatillo Salsa Shrimp Tacos with Leftover Coleslaw

I never liked coleslaw as a child. It was one of the bowls on the picnic table that I would quickly pass by before an adult would insist I "try" it. I am glad my taste buds changed, for leftover coleslaw is a timesaver in the kitchen, especially for Taco Tuesdays.

4 tomatillos
2 poblano peppers, halved, seeded,
   and stemmed
2 Roma tomatoes, halved
1 small onion, quartered
1 red bell pepper, halved, seeded, and
   stemmed
1 jalapeno, halved, seeded, and
   stemmed (optional)

2 cloves garlic
3 tbsp. olive oil, divided
3 tbsp. fresh or 1 tbsp. dried cilantro
Pinch of salt
1 lb. medium shrimp, peeled and
   deveined
Squeeze of lime
10 corn tortillas, white or yellow
1 1/2 cups leftover coleslaw

Preheat oven to 450 degrees.

Husk the tomatillos, and rinse tomatillos under warm water. Dry. Cut in half horizontally.

In a bowl, add all cut vegetables, garlic cloves, and 2 tbsp. olive oil, and toss well. Spread vegetables, cut side down, and garlic in a single layer on a foil-lined baking sheet. Bake for 18-20 minutes.

Remove poblano and red peppers and place in a bowl. Cover with foil and let stand for 10 minutes. Remove skins.

Place all vegetables, peppers, cilantro, and salt in a food processor. Pulse until desired consistency.

In a skillet, over medium-high heat, add remaining 1 tbsp. olive oil and shrimp. Cook for 1 minute.

Stir in tomatillo salsa. Continue to cook until shrimp are pink and fully cooked, 2-3 minutes. Remove from heat. Squeeze with lime.

In a small skillet, over medium-high heat, warm tortillas one at a time for 10 seconds per side. Remove and keep warm. To serve, put tomatillo salsa shrimp mix into warm tortillas and top with leftover coleslaw.

Makes 10 tacos

TO COOK IS TO CREATE: What other vegetables could you roast? Eggplant, carrots, or green bell peppers? Want a little more zing? Add 1 tbsp. tequila during the last 30 seconds of cooking the shrimp. Substitute leftover grilled or boiled shrimp to make this recipe even quicker. How about adding black beans or corn to the coleslaw before using? Other toppings could include avocado slices or guacamole, sour cream, shredded cheese, sliced jalapenos, and sliced black olives.

Tiny Tidbit: Just like leftover coleslaw, don't throw away tossed salad that is getting soft from the dressing. Use it as a topping for a frittata or omelette. It's a nice combo of hot and cold.

Notes:

_____

_____

_____

_____

_____

_____

_____

Crispy Tuna Salad Fritters

Tuna salad—I hated it as a child and still do! The smell always seemed to linger around the table long after the container was closed. Do you know who doesn't hate it? My hubby. He loves it, and it is his go-to lunch when I am out of town. One time upon my return, I opened the fridge and saw a container of tuna salad that Hubby failed to completely consume. My first thought was what on earth was he thinking? He told me he did not get to finish it and could not consider wasting it. Smart man. I began to think about what on earth I could do with the tuna salad. In Louisiana we fry just about anything, so why not this? I may not like tuna salad, but I love fried cod, and these crispy fritters remind me of fish and chips.

⅓ cup self-rising flour, sifted
1 egg
1 green onion, chopped
1 small onion, diced
1 tsp. dried parsley
Black pepper
1 cup leftover tuna salad
Pickle juice, pickled jalapeno juice, or
     water
Oil for frying
Creole seasoning, to taste

For the Sauce:
½ cup Greek yogurt
1 clove garlic, minced
1 tbsp. minced fresh dill with stems
1 tsp. fresh lemon juice
⅛ tsp. celery seed
Lemon wedges (optional)

In a large bowl, combine flour, egg, onions, parsley, and pepper. Gently fold in tuna salad. Add enough pickle juice, pickled jalapeno juice, or water to create a thick batter. Place mixture in refrigerator and let stand for 10 minutes.

In a heavy pot or deep fryer, heat oil to 350 degrees.

Using a cookie scoop, drop fritter batter into hot oil. Fry until golden brown. Remove to paper towels with slotted spoon, sprinkle fritters with Creole seasoning, and let drain.

To make the sauce, combine yogurt, garlic, dill, lemon juice, and celery seed. Serve fritters with sauce and lemon wedges for squeezing, if desired.

Makes 1 dozen

Tiny Tidbit: If you have leftover finger sandwiches from a party, freeze them or make Monte Cristo-type sandwiches. Gently press a sandwich together. Dip each side in a mixture of beaten egg and milk. In a skillet, over medium heat, melt 1 tbsp. butter until foaming. Add sandwich and cook for 4 minutes on first side, flip, then cook an additional 3-4 minutes (or until desired crispness). Top with powdered sugar. Serve with jelly for dipping!

Notes:

_____

_____

_____

_____

_____

_____

_____

_____

BIG CHEESY BISCUITS AND GRAVY

Macaroni, cheese, biscuits, and gravy . . . what's not to love? Some may say there is no such thing as leftover macaroni and cheese. If that's the case in your house, simply "hide" a portion on the side to make these biscuits. Leftover mac and cheese is "cut" into the flour like butter, making these biscuits quite filling. I like the ease of drop biscuits, but if you prefer, the dough can be rolled out on a lightly floured board to 1/3-in. thickness and cut with a small biscuit cutter.

1 cup sifted all-purpose flour
1 tsp. baking powder
1/2 tsp. salt
1 tsp. Creole seasoning
1/2 cup leftover macaroni and cheese
1/3 cup milk
2 tbsp. butter, melted
1/4 cup grated cheddar cheese

For the Cajun Sausage Gravy:
1/4 cup crumbled cooked breakfast
   sausage
1 tbsp. butter
1 tbsp. flour
1 tsp. Creole seasoning
1 cup milk

Preheat oven to 450 degrees.

In a large bowl, sift flour, baking powder, salt, and Creole seasoning. Cut in leftover macaroni and cheese until it resembles fine crumbs. Slowly add milk until soft dough is formed.

Drop by tablespoons onto a parchment-lined baking sheet.

Bake for 12-15 minutes or until golden brown.

Brush with melted butter and sprinkle with cheese.

To make the gravy, in a small saucepan over medium heat, add sausage and butter. Heat until butter is melted. Whisk in flour and Creole seasoning. Keep whisking and slowly add milk. Continue to cook and whisk until gravy is thickened.

Serve gravy on side for dipping or on top of biscuits.

Makes 6 biscuits

TO COOK IS TO CREATE: Not a traditional cheddar macaroni and cheese fan? Use your favorite. Leftover smoked gouda mac and cheese biscuits are another favorite of mine, especially when served with blueberry preserves. Have bacon or pimentos in your leftover mac and cheese? Even better! Want to add fresh herbs? Chives are a good choice. If you don't have breakfast sausage, simply omit or use cooked crumbled bacon, chopped ham, or a leftover crumbled hamburger. Not a biscuits and gravy fan? Serve these biscuits with garlic butter as a side for dinner.

Notes:

_____

_____

_____

_____

_____

_____

_____

LEFTOVER MAC AND CHEESE BREAD

This macaroni and cheese bread is easy to prepare with the help of biscuit mix. I use mayonnaise because I like the richness it adds, just like a rich and creamy mac and cheese, but an egg can easily be substituted.

1 small onion, diced
2 tbsp. butter, divided
1 1/2 cups biscuit mix
1/2 cup grated cheddar cheese, divided

1/2 cup leftover macaroni and cheese
3 tbsp. mayonnaise
3/4 cup milk

Preheat oven to 400 degrees.

Sauté onion in 1 tbsp. butter until soft.

In a mixing bowl, combine biscuit mix, 1/4 cup cheese, and leftover macaroni and cheese. Add mayonnaise and milk. Stir gently, then fold in onions.

Use remaining butter to grease a loaf pan. Pour batter into pan. Sprinkle with remaining cheese.

Bake for 35-40 minutes.

Makes 1 loaf

TO COOK IS TO CREATE: Not an onion fan? Substitute diced bell peppers. No cheddar cheese? Use a cheddar cheese blend, Monterey Jack, Swiss, or Italian shredded cheese blend. Like it spicy? Use pepper Jack or habanero Jack cheese and add some sliced jalapenos. If you're a bacon lover, add crumbled cooked bacon to the batter. Have some fresh chives? Add them. Leftover cooked breakfast sausage? Add it to the batter for a grab-and-go complete breakfast bread. If you're a butter lover, brush melted butter over the hot cooked loaf and sprinkle with extra cheese.

To MeMaw's House We Go

Southern Holiday Classics

Forget over the river and through the woods to Grandmother's house we go. For me it was along the levee and across the neutral ground to MeMaw's house we go. I always loved visiting my MeMaw and Pawsie but especially during the holidays.

Their house just seemed to come alive during the holidays. There were ceramic decorations, made by my Pawsie, prominently displayed throughout the house. I had my favorites that were like old friends I only got to see during the holidays. There was always a selection of treats on different tables throughout the house as well, making it easy to steal a snack if I managed to escape hugging aunts.

The smells of the holidays were like no other—the toasted marshmallows on the sweet potato casserole, the crispy onions on the green bean casserole, the brown-sugar crust on the ham, and the roasted turkey. Just thinking of those smells creates a Norman Rockwell-like scene in my mind.

Holiday traditions, from decorations to special food and drink, are what make holidays so special. Traditions help link generations together and are all about memories—old and new. We had and have our traditions. My Pawsie was always in charge of carving the turkey, which seemed to get bigger and bigger every year. He may have briefly paused, putting down his electric knife and carving fork during this operation, but that by no means meant for someone else to pick them up and resume. The first two cuts or so were easy—the two drumsticks came off first, one for me and one for my brother. I can't tell you about the other precision cuts, for once I got my drumstick, I was a gone pecan, as we like to say. I can tell you, however, that the turkey carcass always became the base for a pot of gumbo the next day, and the hambone went in the freezer to flavor a future pot of white beans.

There were two dishes that I looked forward to the most. One was my aunt Doris's Swedish meatballs. I would stalk the door waiting for Aunt Doris to arrive with her covered bowl of bite-sized treasures. If I hurried to help her carry it into the kitchen, I almost always got one to taste before anyone else. Sometimes I was even gifted with my own bowl of them.

The other was MeMaw's oyster cornbread dressing. Just writing those words makes my eyes tear and my mouth water. It is the one recipe I wish she would have written down. Since she has been gone, I have tried each year to recreate her dressing. Once I created it close enough to make my mom and aunt say it was her dressing, but I disagreed. I guess I like the challenge each year of getting it MeMaw perfect. In my family, we have always called it dressing not stuffing.

One tradition in my family that still happens is that everyone brings a can of cranberry sauce, just in case. I guess you can say we are a cranberry sauce loving family, the canned kind. Yes, I'm talking about that congealed jelly log that seems to wiggle for at least a minute after being released like a prisoner from the can. At least it is easy to serve—open a can, slide the log out onto a dish (some like

Pawsie doing his ritual carving of the turkey, with me and my brother, Rich, eagerly waiting to steal our turkey legs.

it in a bowl, others on a plate . . . so we do both), and strategically place a butter knife on the side. Then a family member has the honor of cutting the first slice of cranberry sauce. After that, it is fun to sit back and observe the cranberry sauce to turkey ratio on everybody's plate. I now have the honor of MeMaw's place as host and have enjoyed holiday traditions passed down from generation to generation, becoming precious pearls in our memories. I have also learned to embrace the extra cans of cranberry sauce that everyone brings. I would never think to waste them, because after all, it takes about 200 cranberries to make one can.

CRANBERRY SAUCE GLAZE

This easy, sweet, fruity glaze is quick to whisk together and makes a nice seasonal treat when brushed onto hot biscuits. It also can be used as a topping for baked Brie. Either orange juice or apple juice can be added, but my favorite is champagne!

¼ cup leftover cranberry sauce
¼ cup powdered sugar

1 tbsp. orange juice, apple juice, or champagne

In a small bowl, whisk together leftover cranberry sauce and sugar. Slowly whisk in juice or champagne. Brush onto hot biscuits.

Tiny Tidbit: An almost empty jar of jelly can be the base for a glaze, too. Simply add a little powdered sugar and orange juice to the jar and give it a good shake.

CRANBERRY SAUCE SORBET

This sorbet is a great way to use up any leftover cranberry sauce, homemade or canned, as well as any remaining marshmallows from holiday cooking.

12 large or 24 mini marshmallows
1 cup leftover or canned cranberry sauce

1 tbsp. orange juice

In a saucepan, over low heat, add marshmallows and cranberry sauce. Using a rubber spatula, fold cranberry sauce over marshmallows to melt marshmallows. Continue folding until smooth and fluffy. Remove from heat. Let cool for 30 seconds.

Stir orange juice into marshmallow mixture and blend thoroughly.

Pour mixture into a shallow tray. Cover and freeze, stirring twice the first hour. Leave in freezer overnight.

Scoop and serve.

Makes 4 scoops

CRANBERRY SAUCE SIMPLE SYRUP

This recipe is a good way to take a can of jellied cranberry sauce that a guest brought and whip it into a cocktail to serve.

½ cup leftover canned cranberry sauce   1 cup water
1 cup sugar

In a saucepan, over medium heat, add leftover canned cranberry sauce, sugar, and water. Stir until cranberry sauce is melted and sugar is dissolved, about 8-10 minutes. Let cool.

Use in cocktails. Refrigerate any unused portion for up to 2 weeks.

CRANBERRY SAUCE MOJITO

Cranberry sauce makes a wonderful simple syrup to use as a base for holiday cocktails.

2 oz. light rum   2 oz. soda water
2 oz. Cranberry Sauce Simple Syrup   Squeeze of lime
   (see recipe above)   Mint sprig (optional)

Pour rum and Cranberry Sauce Simple Syrup into a tall glass. Stir. Fill glass with ice.

Add soda water and squeeze of lime. Add mint sprig, if using. Sip and enjoy.

CRANBERRY SAUCE CHAMPAGNE COCKTAIL

Here is another one of my favorite concoctions using leftover canned cranberry sauce.

2 oz. vodka   2 oz. champagne
½ oz. Cranberry Sauce Simple Syrup   Lemon twist
   (see recipe above)

Add vodka and Cranberry Sauce Simple Syrup to a cocktail shaker. Fill with ice. Cover and shake.

Strain into a champagne flute. Top with champagne. Run lemon twist around rim of flute, then drop in. Sip and enjoy.

Stuffed Chicken with Creamy Cranberry Brie Sauce

What's the easiest thing about this stuffed chicken? It uses leftover dressing. The sauce is also great on leftover turkey or baked pork chops. I have also been known to ladle this creamy goodness over toast, biscuits, and crepes.

4 boneless, skinless chicken breasts
4 oz. Brie, cubed, rinds reserved
1 cup leftover dressing
1 egg, beaten
1 cup Italian breadcrumbs
2 tbsp. butter
1 tbsp. flour

$1/4$ tsp. white pepper
Dash of salt
$1/8$ tsp. nutmeg
1 cup whole milk
$1 1/2$ tsp. brandy
$1/2$ cup leftover canned cranberry
    sauce

Preheat oven to 350 degrees.

Flatten chicken breasts. Chop Brie rind and mix with the leftover dressing. Spread each chicken breast with $1/4$ cup dressing mixture.

Roll each chicken breast tightly and secure with a toothpick. Add egg and breadcrumbs to separate bowls. Dip each chicken breast in egg, then into breadcrumbs. Place chicken, seam side down, in a lightly greased shallow baking dish.

Bake for 35 minutes or until juices run clear and internal temperature is 165 degrees.

In a saucepan, over medium heat, melt butter. Whisk in flour, pepper, salt, and nutmeg. Continue to whisk until thick and smooth.

Gradually whisk in milk and brandy. Continue to whisk until mixture bubbles.

Whisk in leftover canned cranberry sauce. Continue to whisk for 1 minute. Add cubed Brie. Keep whisking until cheese is melted.

Slice chicken breasts and top with sauce.

Serves 4

TO COOK IS TO CREATE: No Brie? Use Swiss. What other flavors would complement this sauce? How about orange zest, cinnamon, or ginger? If you don't have brandy, substitute an orange liqueur or triple sec.

Chewy Coconut Cranberry Sauce Muffins

These muffins are not too sweet, which is one of the reasons why I like to have them as a snack with a cup of tea.

3 tbsp. butter, softened
3-4 tbsp. sugar
1 egg
1/2 tbsp. lemon juice
3/4 cup flour
3/4 tsp. baking powder

1/4 tsp. salt
3/4 cup leftover canned cranberry sauce
1/2 cup chopped nuts
1/4 cup coconut flakes
Powdered sugar, for topping (optional)

Preheat oven to 350 degrees.

Using a wooden spoon, cream together butter and sugar (amount depending on desired sweetness) until light and fluffy. Add egg and lemon juice. Beat until smooth.

In a separate bowl, sift together flour, baking powder, and salt. Add to butter mixture.

Cut in pieces of leftover canned cranberry sauce. Gently incorporate. Fold in nuts and coconut.

Drop mixture by tablespoons into each well of a nonstick mini muffin tin. Bake for 20 minutes until top springs back or a toothpick comes out clean. Remove and dust with powdered sugar, if desired.

Makes 24

TO COOK IS TO CREATE: Have any chocolate chips or baking chocolate? Mix in the chips before baking, or melt the chocolate and drizzle on top of cooked muffins. Like to spice things up? Add 1/2-1 tsp. of your favorite spice—cinnamon, ginger, nutmeg, allspice. If you like it zesty, add orange or lemon zest. What else could you add? Poppy seeds or dried fruit? Nut choices include pecans, walnuts, pistachios, almonds, or macadamias. Not a coconut lover? Just omit it.

Club Sandwich Meatballs

While standing in line to pick up the holiday ham one year, I had the most delightful conversations regarding leftover ham. The most mentioned use for it was in a club sandwich. Let's face it. There's nothing wrong with a leftover ham sandwich—make mine hot on buttered toast, please! The second most mentioned use was the old-fashioned ham meatballs with brown sugar glaze recipe. That's a good standby, too. I always add brandy and orange preserves to my glaze. The talk of club sandwiches and ham meatballs set my mind in motion. What if I could combine the recipes? I did, and these turkey, ham, and bacon meatballs were the result. I like a side of honey mustard with a club sandwich, so I finish these club meatballs with a honey-mustard glaze.

½ lb. ground turkey*
6 slices bacon, cooked and crumbled
1 slice bread, toasted
1 tbsp. mayonnaise
½ lb. leftover ham

1 tsp. dry mustard
1 tsp. garlic powder
¼ cup honey
1 tbsp. Creole mustard
1 tsp. prepared horseradish (optional)

Preheat oven to 400 degrees.

Place ground turkey and crumbled bacon in a bowl.

Spread toast with mayonnaise, and slice. Place slices in a food processor along with ham. Process until minced.

Add mixture to turkey and bacon, along with mustard and garlic powder. Using moistened hands, blend well. Take 1 heaping tbsp. mixture and roll into a ball. Repeat with remaining mixture.

Place balls into each well of a nonstick mini muffin tin. (You will have enough for 18 balls.) Bake for 15 minutes. Let cool for 5 minutes.

In a small mixing bowl, blend honey, Creole mustard, and horseradish. Liberally brush mixture onto the meatballs. Broil for 5 minutes.

Makes 18 meatballs

*Leftover cooked turkey can be used. Simply mince in a food processor.

TO COOK IS TO CREATE: Start with what you enjoy on your club sandwich and go from there. Avocado? Mash and add to mixture. Cheese? Cube and stuff each meatball. If you like *chicken* clubs, use ground chicken instead of turkey.

Ham and Sweet Potato Tots

I don't know what it is about tater tots, but I always feel like a kid when I eat them. Perhaps it's because no utensils are required, making them easy to pop into my mouth. These simple tater tots are done in under 20 minutes and transition effortlessly from breakfast to brunch, lunch, or dinner. These are not your average little tots—they are hearty. I wanted to do a dipping sauce for this recipe, but the ones I like with these tots vary from meal to meal. For instance, for breakfast, I enjoy the tots with apple butter. For brunch, I like them with a poached egg and a dollop of orange marmalade. For lunch, they are heavenly when lined up in a hot dog bun with some spicy mustard. For dinner, serve them as is, as a perfect side.

1 cup cooked ground ham
2 cups leftover mashed sweet
   potatoes
1 egg, beaten

¾ cup all-purpose flour
1 tsp. baking powder
½ tsp. salt
Nonstick cooking or olive oil spray

Preheat oven to 350 degrees.

In a bowl, combine ham, sweet potatoes, and egg.

Sift flour, baking powder, and salt together and add to ham mixture. Using a wooden spoon, gently fold together until dough is formed.

Using moistened hands, take dough by teaspoons, and roll each into a ball. Spray nonstick cooking or olive oil spray into each well of 2 mini muffin tins. (You will have enough dough for 36 balls.) Place balls into greased tins.

Bake for 10 minutes. Using a spoon, gently flip each tot. Bake an additional 5 minutes.

Makes 36

Tiny Tidbit: If you have leftover ham slices, spread one or both sides with Dijon mustard or favorite mustard and coat with crushed crackers. In a skillet, over medium-high heat, sauté in equal parts butter and olive oil until brown. Think fried pork chops!

Sweet Potato Casserole Cornbread

Using leftover sweet potato casserole with pecans, cinnamon, and marshmallows makes this cornbread extra nice for a morning treat with a cup of coffee.

2 cups self-rising cornmeal
$\frac{1}{4}$ tsp. salt
1 tbsp. self-rising flour
1 egg, beaten
1 cup whole milk or half-and-half

1 cup leftover sweet potato
   casserole
1 tsp. canola oil
1 tsp. butter

Preheat oven to 350 degrees.

In a mixing bowl, whisk cornmeal, salt, and self-rising flour with egg and milk. Fold in the leftover sweet potato casserole.

In a cast-iron skillet, add the oil and butter. Place in heated oven for 5 minutes. Remove.

Carefully scrape cornbread mixture into hot cast-iron skillet.

Bake for 20 minutes or until a toothpick comes out clean.

Tiny Tidbit: Use leftover sweet potato casserole to make a whipped butter. Using a wooden spoon, whip $\frac{1}{4}$ cup leftover sweet potato casserole into 2 tbsp. softened butter until fluffy. Enjoy slathered over hot cornbread, spread on biscuits or toast, or stirred into grits (my favorite) or oatmeal. It freezes well, too.

SWEET POTATO STUFFED APPLES

I didn't even realize I liked sweet potatoes combined with apples until a couple of years ago at a dinner gathering, when the host served a baked apple and sweet potato casserole. I was pleasantly surprised by the mildly sweet flavors. I am thankful to the host for inspiring a new leftover tradition.

1 apple, halved and cored*
1 tbsp. plus 1 tsp. brown sugar,
    divided
1 tsp. maple syrup
¼ cup apple juice

1 tbsp. bourbon
2 tbsp. butter, divided
1 tbsp. heavy cream or half-and-half
1 cup leftover sweet potato
    casserole

Preheat oven to 400 degrees.

Place apple halves, cut side up, in a shallow baking dish. Sprinkle 1 tsp. brown sugar over apple halves and drizzle with maple syrup. Mix apple juice and bourbon and pour around apple halves.

Bake for 20 minutes, spooning liquid over apple halves every 10 minutes. Let cool enough to handle.

Scoop out apple halves, leaving 2 shells. Mince pulp and transfer warm pulp to a bowl. Mix in 1 tbsp. butter until melted, then stir in cream and leftover sweet potato casserole. Using a whisk or electric hand mixer, beat mixture until fluffy.

Fill each apple shell with mixture and return to baking dish. Sprinkle with remaining brown sugar and dot with remaining butter. Return to oven and bake for 5 minutes.

*Add apple core to a 1-qt. saucepan. Cover with 1 cup water. Bring to a boil, then simmer for 30 minutes. Strain. Use juice for the apple juice in this recipe, or use to make hot tea.

TO COOK IS TO CREATE: Love cinnamon? Add with the brown sugar before baking apples. No nuts in the leftover casserole? Toss some toasted ones into potato mixture. If you have any leftover cranberries, add them. Feeling tropical? Add toasted coconut and chopped pineapple to potato mixture. Marshmallow lover? Add some to top along with the brown sugar and butter.

HOT GREEN BEAN CASSEROLE ONION DIP

This hot "casserole to company" dip is a seasonal favorite of mine. The inspiration for this recipe came from combining two classic dips, spinach and artichoke and caramelized onion. I use leftover green bean casserole as the "spinach" and add a blend of cheeses, bacon, artichoke hearts, and caramelized onions for a dip worthy of company. If you have some crispy onions left over from your casserole, sprinkle them on top of this dip before baking. When I eat onion dip, I choose a ruffled potato chip, and that's my favorite vessel for enjoying this dip, too.

2 strips bacon
1 medium yellow onion, thinly sliced
1 clove garlic, minced
$\frac{1}{2}$ tsp. light brown sugar
4 oz. cream cheese, softened
2 tbsp. mayonnaise
1 tbsp. grated Parmesan cheese
$\frac{1}{4}$ cup shredded mozzarella cheese, divided

7-oz. can baby artichoke hearts, drained* and chopped
$\frac{1}{8}$ tsp. white pepper
$\frac{1}{4}$ tsp. Worcestershire sauce
$\frac{1}{2}$ cup leftover green bean casserole, roughly chopped

In a cast-iron skillet, cook bacon. Remove bacon to a paper-towel-lined plate to cool. Crumble.

In the skillet with the bacon fat, over medium-low heat, cook onions, garlic, and brown sugar, stirring often until onions are golden brown, about 15 minutes.

Preheat oven to 350 degrees.

In a medium bowl, blend cream cheese, mayonnaise, Parmesan cheese, half of mozzarella cheese, artichoke hearts, pepper, Worcestershire, crumbled bacon, onions, and leftover green bean casserole. Pour mixture into a lightly greased $1\frac{1}{2}$-2-qt. baking dish. Sprinkle with remaining mozzarella cheese.

Bake for 15 minutes or until golden brown. Serve with chips.

*Juice from artichokes can be blended with olive oil and minced garlic and used as a bread dip.

Green Bean Casserole Fries

If you like fried green beans, you will devour these as quickly as you can make them. I love to dip them in the accompanying spicy Dijon mustard sauce.

$\frac{1}{2}$ cup leftover green bean casserole
1 cup leftover mashed potatoes
1 tbsp. all-purpose flour
Oil for frying

2 tbsp. Dijon mustard
1 tbsp. honey
$\frac{3}{4}$ tsp. prepared horseradish

Place leftover green bean casserole in a mini food processor. Pulse into a puree.

Mix puree with leftover mashed potatoes. Gradually add the flour to make a thick batter.

Heat oil to 350 degrees.

Transfer mixture to a piping bag. Pipe directly into hot oil. Fry for 1 minute. Remove with a slotted spoon to drain.

In a small bowl, add Dijon mustard. Whisk in honey and horseradish. Serve on side for dipping.

Creamy Crab Mashed Potato au Gratin

I love crabmeat au gratin, but I definitely do not like the cost usually associated with making it. This recipe takes a little bit of crabmeat and stretches it with the help of leftover mashed potatoes. Fully loaded or garlic mashed potatoes make this dish even tastier.

1 cup leftover mashed potatoes	$\frac{1}{4}$ tsp. Worcestershire sauce
1 $\frac{1}{2}$ tbsp. butter, divided	$\frac{1}{8}$ tsp. Louisiana hot sauce
1 tbsp. flour	1 cup flaked crabmeat*
$\frac{1}{4}$ tsp. Creole seasoning	$\frac{1}{4}$ cup shredded cheddar Jack
$\frac{1}{2}$ cup milk	$\frac{1}{4}$ cup breadcrumbs
1 tsp. brandy	1 tsp. grated Parmesan cheese

Preheat oven to 350 degrees. Lightly grease 4 (4-oz.) ramekins.

Add $\frac{1}{4}$ cup leftover mashed potatoes to each ramekin. Using the back of a spoon, press mashed potatoes into bottom and up sides of each ramekin. Set aside.

In a small saucepan, over medium heat, melt 1 tbsp. butter. Blend in flour and Creole seasoning, stirring until smooth. Gradually whisk in milk. Bring to a boil.

Whisk in brandy, Worcestershire sauce, and hot sauce. Cook for 1 minute.

Add crabmeat. Continue to cook an additional 1-2 minutes or until thickened. Remove from heat. Stir in cheddar Jack. Keep stirring until cheese is well blended.

In a small skillet, melt remaining butter. Stir in breadcrumbs and cook until lightly toasted. Remove from heat. Mix in Parmesan cheese.

Add crabmeat cheese sauce to each ramekin and top with buttered breadcrumbs.

Bake for 15 minutes.

*Can substitute $\frac{1}{2}$ cup chopped cooked shrimp or crawfish tails for the crabmeat.

Tiny Tidbit: Use leftover mashed potatoes in ramekins when making baked eggs.

Potato au Gratin Puffs with Brandy Cream Sauce

Potatoes au gratin bring together two of my favorites, potatoes and cheese, and make them even better with cream. Gruyère cheese is one of the cheeses I use for potatoes au gratin as it pairs well with brandy! No, I don't have a glass of brandy when I eat potatoes au gratin (although it does sound good), but I do use it in my cream sauce. I always add brandy and a little Dijon, which really elevate the flavor. I absolutely love the crispy, cheesy edges of an au gratin. If you like that, too, then you will adore these. These puffs are great for using up the bits of cheese and last bites of mashed potatoes that you didn't think were worth saving. Try these for brunch alongside scrambled eggs.

1 1/2 tbsp. leftover mashed potatoes
1 tbsp. ricotta cheese
1 tbsp. grated Gruyère cheese
1/2 tsp. chopped fresh herbs (dill, rosemary, thyme, or chives)
1 roll refrigerated piecrust
1 tbsp. heavy cream

For the Sauce:
1/4 cup brandy
1/2 cup heavy cream
1/2 tsp. Dijon mustard
1/4 cup grated Gruyère cheese

Preheat oven to 350 degrees.

In a small bowl, mix leftover mashed potatoes, cheeses, and herbs.

Using a rolling pin, roll out piecrust. With a 2-in. biscuit cutter, cut rounds from crust. Keep rolling out the scraps and cutting rounds until all the crust has been used.

Drop 1/2 tsp. potato mixture onto each round. Fold round over potato filling. Using your fingers, press in filling, and with a fork, crimp edges of crust to seal.

Place puffs onto a parchment-lined baking sheet. Brush puffs with cream. Bake for 15 minutes.

To make the sauce, in a small saucepan, over low heat, whisk together brandy, cream, mustard, and Gruyère cheese. Continue to whisk until the cheese is melted and the sauce begins to thicken. Remove from heat.

Drizzle puffs with sauce or serve sauce on side for dipping.

Makes 20 puffs

Tiny Tidbit: If you still have leftover ricotta cheese, brush a pizza crust with olive oil, and then spread on ricotta to make a quick base for pizza toppings.

Dressy Ravioli

Wonton wrappers are my secret holiday weapon for leftovers. I always make sure I have a package in the fridge. They can be filled with leftovers and made into fried wontons, wonton soup, pot stickers, or—my favorite—ravioli. It is important to work quickly with the wrappers, so have all ingredients ready to go. I call this Dressy Ravioli because the dressing-filled "pasta" gets all dressed up in a brown butter mushroom sage sauce.

24 wonton wrappers
1 ½ cups leftover dressing
1 tsp. salt
1 tsp. olive oil
8 oz. fresh mushrooms, chopped

1 shallot, diced
4 sage leaves, rolled and sliced
4 tbsp. unsalted butter, sliced
Freshly grated Parmesan cheese and
   black pepper for serving

Add water to a small dish. Working one by one, lay a wrapper on a clean work surface. Using your finger or a pastry brush, cover entire side (not just the edges) of a wrapper with water.

Place 1 tbsp. dressing in the center of the wrapper.

Pick up another wrapper and brush water along all 4 edges. Place moistened side over filling. Using your fingers, press down around filling and work towards the edges, pushing out air to create a tight seal. The ravioli can be kept square or cut into shapes using a pastry wheel or ravioli stamp. (If cut, use leftover "scraps" in a soup, or fry for a salad topping.)

Bring a large pot of water to a boil. Add the salt. Reduce heat to simmer.

Gently drop in ravioli one by one, to prevent sticking, and *do not crowd the pot* (cook in a few batches if needed). Cook ravioli for 2-3 minutes or until they float to the top. Remove with a slotted spoon to warm serving bowls or plates.

In a skillet, over medium heat, drizzle olive oil. Add mushrooms, shallot, and sage leaves. Sauté for 5 minutes. Set skillet aside.

In a stainless-steel saucepan, over medium-low heat, begin to melt butter slowly (low and slow). Keep stirring or swirling saucepan constantly. The butter will begin to foam. Watch closely. When the butter turns *amber*, immediately pour it into the skillet with the mushroom mixture, and stir.

Serve sauce over ravioli. Top with freshly grated Parmesan cheese and black pepper.

Serves 4

Tiny Tidbit: Leftover mashed butternut squash, or acorn squash casserole, can be used as a wonton filling, too.

Notes:

_____

_____

_____

_____

_____

_____

_____

Stuffed Breakfast Rolls

This recipe was my first leftover dressing creation. It is a dish I look forward to each year. I usually make it with my signature shrimp and eggplant dressing. I love that it can be wrapped and eaten warm on the run, whether I am out shopping or visiting friends or family.

4 leftover dinner rolls	1 tsp. Italian seasoning
2 eggs	¼ cup leftover dressing
2 tsp. half-and-half or heavy cream	2 tbsp. grated cheese

Preheat oven to 350 degrees.

Lightly grease 4 wells of a muffin tin. Place rolls into wells and gently press down.

Whisk eggs with half-and-half or cream. Pour egg mixture over wells, reserving half. Let sit for 5 minutes.

Sprinkle seasoning over rolls. Top each with 1 tbsp. leftover dressing, pressing down with back of spoon. Pour remaining egg mixture over rolls, and top with cheese.

Bake for 20-25 minutes or until center is set and bounces back when pressed. Slide butter knife around each well to remove rolls and enjoy.

TO COOK IS TO CREATE: Think about all the different dressings and how each would make a unique breakfast roll. Want more flavor? Substitute flavored cream or eggnog. Want heartier breakfast rolls? Add some diced leftover ham or turkey or crumbled bacon. If you like it spicy, toss in jalapenos, hot sauce, or pepper Jack cheese. Does your dressing contain nuts? If not, top rolls with toasted pecans or walnuts before adding eggs. No leftover rolls? Use the dressing as the "cup." Simply place a layer of dressing into each well, and press down and up sides before adding egg mix.

Pie Baked Brie

If I need a quick appetizer to serve unexpected guests during the holidays, this is it. We always seem to have a pie in the house, so I make sure I have Brie in the fridge. A slice of pecan, peach, or apple pie makes a quick topping for baked Brie.

1 slice leftover pecan, peach, or apple pie
8-oz. wheel Brie

1 tbsp. honey
$1/3$ cup chopped pecans or walnuts
Crackers for serving

Preheat oven to 350 degrees.

Place slice of leftover pie in a food processor. Pulse a few times to make a pie "puree."

Line an oven-safe dish with parchment paper, cut to fit if needed.

Use a knife to score the top of the Brie, and place in the dish. Drizzle with honey. Spread the pie "puree" over the Brie, and top with pecans or walnuts.

Bake for 10-12 minutes until the Brie is soft. Let sit for 2 minutes before enjoying with crackers.

Serves 4

Pecan-Pie Baked Salmon

This is my never-fail-to-impress-guests recipe. It turns plain baked salmon into a conversation piece, because no one can ever guess the secret ingredient until I divulge that it is pecan pie.

1 slice leftover pecan pie
2 skinless salmon fillets, 6 oz. each
1 tbsp. maple syrup

$\frac{1}{2}$ cup chopped pecans
1 tbsp. light brown sugar

Preheat oven to 400 degrees.

Place leftover pecan pie in a food processor. Pulse a few times to make a pie "puree."

Rinse salmon fillets and pat dry. Place on a parchment-lined baking sheet. Drizzle maple syrup over salmon fillets.

Spread pecan pie "puree" evenly over each salmon fillet. Mix pecans with brown sugar and sprinkle over fillets.

Bake for 10-12 minutes until salmon flakes easily with a fork.

Serves 2

Tiny Tidbit: Mix pecan pie "puree" with chopped pecans and use as a shortcut sweet potato casserole topping.

Swiss Apple Pie Mini Quiche

I modeled this recipe after a baked apple and Swiss cheese tart that I savored while sipping a fruit brandy in a little bakery in Basel, Switzerland. I loved the way the sweet apples highlighted the nuttiness of the freshly sliced Swiss cheese. One day I happened to have a slice of apple pie and some Swiss cheese in the fridge. Recalling that October day in the bakery, I wondered if I could combine what I had on hand to mimic the flavors of my beloved tart. This crustless quiche delivered. I love the texture of the piecrust baked with the egg mixture. This recipe also works well with peach pie.

1 slice leftover apple pie (4-4½ oz.)
2 slices Swiss cheese
1 egg
½ cup milk or half-and-half

⅛ tsp. cinnamon
⅛ tsp. nutmeg
Shredded Parmesan cheese, for
   topping (optional)

Preheat oven to 375 degrees. Lightly grease a 5-in. individual tart pan or pie dish.

Place leftover apple pie in bottom of pan. Using a fork, break up pie to cover bottom of pan.

Tear Swiss cheese slices to cover pie mixture.

Whisk together egg, milk or half-and-half, cinnamon, and nutmeg. Pour over pie and cheese.

Bake for 25-30 minutes or until center is set. Cool slightly before cutting into wedges. Top with shredded Parmesan cheese, if desired.

Serves 1

   Tiny Tidbit: If you have leftover ham, add 1 or 2 slices with the Swiss cheese.

"Curry Me Away" Apple Pie Chutney

I always make an apple chutney ahead of time in anticipation of leftover turkey or ham. One year, the apple I had set aside to use was mistakenly eaten for breakfast. I worried I was going to have to go without my leftover tradition. However, I put on my "To Cook Is to Create" thinking cap and used a slice of apple pie instead. The result was a new and improved relish and a keeper. I love Indian food, and the aroma and flavor of this simple chutney delight my senses and carry my tastes buds away. It not only awakens leftover turkey and ham but also leftover pork chops. It is a definite game changer for a turkey sandwich, too.

1 tbsp. apple juice
1 tbsp. dark rum
2 tbsp. light brown sugar

1 slice leftover apple pie (4-4$\frac{1}{2}$ oz.)
3 tbsp. raisins
$\frac{1}{4}$ tsp. Madras curry powder

In a small saucepan, over medium heat, pour apple juice and dark rum. Whisk in brown sugar, and keep whisking for 1 minute.

Chop up the leftover apple pie. Stir into the saucepan, along with raisins and curry powder. Reduce heat to low.

Simmer for 5 minutes. Remove from heat and let cool. Chill in fridge for at least 1 hour or overnight.

Serve with leftover ham or turkey slices.

Makes $\frac{1}{2}$ cup

TO COOK IS TO CREATE: No dark rum? Use brandy. Want to omit the alcohol? Replace with more apple juice, or use orange juice. If you don't have raisins, substitute dried cranberries or chopped dried apricots. No curry powder? Use $\frac{1}{8}$ tsp. each ground cumin and ginger. Have some chopped walnuts or pecans? Stir them in at the end. If you don't want to chill the chutney, enjoy it at room temperature on a charcuterie board or in a grilled cheese sandwich.

A Little Something Sweet

One More Sliver of Pie

With my family and friends, anytime someone says they will have "one more sliver of pie," you can bet that their definition of a sliver is not a "small thin piece of something" as stated in the *Oxford English Dictionary*. I consider "one more sliver of pie" to simply be a polite Southern response to a host offering another serving of dessert. It could probably be replaced with: "I'm way too full, but maybe just a small slice." Even with that, I notice that the marking cut with the knife starts off small and ends up being a regular slice—or larger. Just once, I would like to hear someone say they will have one large hunk or slab of pie. I'm sure the response would be applause or cheers, almost like the crowd cheering on competitive eaters.

I am not much of a sweets person and can often pass up dessert, so going back for "one more sliver of pie" has never been a statement from me. I will, however, proudly state that I will take home any pie that no one wishes to consume. Notice I did not say "leftover" pie. I try to avoid that, for every single time I have ever uttered it or typed it, I have gotten numerous comments that there is no such thing as leftover pie. So, the recipes in this chapter do not use leftover pie; rather, they utilize "excess" pie.

There is no saying about going back for cookies or taking "a few cookies for later." If there were, I would definitely be guilty of saying it. I may be able to pass on most desserts but never on cookies. To me, cookies are freebies, as in I'm free to eat a few and not feel guilty.

LEFTOVER PIE DOUGH COOKIES

Whether I have a roll of prepared pie dough or some pie dough scraps, this is my go-to way to use it up along with any cookies I have in the pantry. This recipe is a lifesaver for any stale cookies. Pie dough and cookies . . . that is it, until you put on your "To Cook Is to Create" thinking cap, of course. For instance, a favorite combination of mine is chocolate sandwich cookies with macadamia nuts and flaked sea salt.

2-4 cookies   Leftover pie dough

Preheat oven to 400 degrees.

Crumble cookies into a food processor. Process until they resemble breadcrumbs.

Roll out leftover pie dough into a rectangle. Sprinkle cookie crumbs onto the dough. Using a rolling pin, roll over crumbs once, pushing them into the dough. Starting at shortest end, roll up the dough. Chill for 10 minutes.

Slice dough into rounds 1/2 in. thick. Place on a parchment-lined baking sheet.

Bake for 12 minutes.

TO COOK IS TO CREATE: Use this as a base recipe to make a variety of cookie flavors. Nuts or candy can be added to the processor with the cookies. Don't forget to spice it up. For example, process shortbread cookies with pecans and cinnamon, or vanilla wafers with walnuts and ground ginger and cloves. Melted chocolate can be drizzled on baked cookies, too.

Uses for "Excess" Pie

The key to all these "excess" pie possibilities is pie puree. It works well with just about any pie. Pecan, fruit, pumpkin, custard, cream, key lime—you name it.

1 slice excess pie

Place slice of excess pie in a food processor. Pulse a few times to make a pie "puree."

Uses for pecan or berry pie purees:
   Mix into hot oatmeal.
   Mix with cream cheese for bagel spread.
   Use pecan pie puree as is for a biscuit spread.
   Blend with butter for spreading onto hot muffins or toast.
   Stir into icing for cupcakes or cookies.
   Mix into pancake or waffle batter.

Uses for custard or cream pie purees:
   Whip into heavy cream or mascarpone cheese as a filling for crepes.
   Use as a filling for baked cupcakes or topping for pound cakes.

Uses for chocolate cream pie puree:
   Make my favorite: pie-filled doughnuts. Chocolate cream pie puree makes a doughnut taste just like an éclair! To make these "doughnuts," use refrigerated biscuits (not flaky). Separate biscuits. Deep fry until brown, 1-2 minutes. Roll in sugar or powdered sugar. Poke hole in side of doughnuts. Fill a pastry bag fitted with a small decorating tip with the pie puree. Fill the doughnuts. Refrigerate any leftovers. These are delicious when served warm: reheat for 10 seconds in the microwave.

Pie milkshakes:
   This works well with just about *any* pie! Here's a quick guide, but amounts will depend on your preference for a thicker (more ice cream) or thinner (more milk) milkshake. Place 1 slice excess pie in blender or use pie puree. Add 3 scoops softened ice cream and $1/4$ cup milk. Process until smooth or until desired consistency. Top with whipped cream.
   Think of how many kinds of milkshake you can make with different pies and ice creams. Here are some of my favorite combinations to inspire you: sweet potato pie and butter pecan ice cream; apple pie and caramel swirl ice cream; pumpkin pie and pralines and cream ice cream; pecan pie and chocolate fudge ice cream, like

a chocolate fudge pecan pie. During the holidays I enjoy a milkshake of pecan pie and French vanilla ice cream with eggnog instead of milk.

TO COOK IS TO CREATE: For milkshakes, think about what else can be put in the blender with the pie, ice cream, and milk for added flavor—nuts, syrups, extracts, spices. The flavors, such as maple syrup, caramel, bourbon, or Kahlua, should complement the pie. What other uses can you think of for pie puree? If you ask my mom, she will say, "All you need is a spoon!"

Notes:

Leftover Mashed Potato Almond Torte with Whipped Lemon Curd

Every chef, recipe developer, and food blogger spends test days in the kitchen. I love test days, except for the countless dirty dishes that seem to accumulate every time I turn my back. Test days are full of excitement and suspense. They are a "come to life" moment for an idea—an idea that, for me, has usually kept my mind spinning when I try to go to sleep. When I think of all the different components of a new dish, my idea can almost deliver the taste or, should I say, the expected taste. Everyone who has had test days knows that not all are successes. Even with disappointing test days, I always learn something, making it all worthwhile. On the other hand, successful test days make me do a happy dance in the kitchen. The dance usually begins as I anxiously take the first bite and my taste buds erupt with affirmation. When I tested this torte, it was a successful test day. I always call my mom to tell her the good news. I definitely phoned her that day, for I was testing this torte recipe for her. Those who know me know that I am not a baker, but I wanted to make something special for my mom. I needed something to present for my television segment, and I wanted to make a dish that had my mom's favorite whipped lemon curd in it. I decided to do a segment on leftover mashed potatoes, and that is how the whole thing started. Since I knew that leftover mashed potatoes make wonderful scones and bread, I wondered about other baked goods. A torte? Yes!

1 tbsp. butter, melted
1 tbsp. flour for dusting pan
4 eggs, lightly beaten
$2/3$ cup sugar
$1/3$ cup plus 1 tbsp. all-purpose flour
$1/2$ tsp. baking powder
Pinch of salt

2 tsp. lemon zest
$1/2$ cup ground almonds
$1/3$ cup leftover mashed potatoes
1 jar lemon curd
1 cup heavy cream
Powdered sugar, for topping
   (optional)

Preheat oven to 350 degrees.

Brush an 8-in. round cake pan or torte pan with melted butter. If using cake pan, line with greased parchment paper. Dust pan with flour, and shake off excess.

In a large mixing bowl, using an electric hand mixer, beat eggs and sugar until thick and glossy. Sift together flour, baking powder, and salt. Fold into egg mixture with lemon zest, almonds, and leftover mashed potatoes. Mix lightly.

Spread mixture into pan. Bake for 40-45 minutes or until lightly golden and torte has shrunk from sides of pan. Let rest for 5 minutes. Turn onto a wire rack to cool.

In a bowl, using a rubber spatula, stir lemon curd until smooth.

Add cream to a chilled bowl. Whip until it doubles in volume and forms soft peaks. Gently stir a little whipped cream into lemon curd before folding in the remaining cream.

Split torte horizontally. Spread a torte layer with lemon cream. Top with remaining torte layer. Dust with powdered sugar, if desired.

TO COOK IS TO CREATE: No lemon? Use orange or lime zest. Not an almond fan? Use ground pecans or walnuts. If you have a favorite berry, add it to the lemon curd filling, or top the torte as a garnish.

Notes:

_____

_____

_____

_____

_____

_____

_____

_____

LEFTOVER CINNAMON-ROLL PUMPKIN-SPICE CHEESECAKES

Pumpkin spice, the official flavor of fall . . . yes, I'm a spice girl! I buy just about anything labeled "pumpkin spice." Every autumn I have pumpkin-spice lip balm in my purse, pumpkin-spice candy corn on my desk, pumpkin-spice coffee and pumpkin-spice biscotti in the cupboard along with pumpkin-spice creamer in the fridge, and maybe a few chocolate-caramel pumpkin-spice truffles hidden away for safekeeping. After I made these cheesecakes one day, they quickly became my new pumpkin-spice obsession. Using leftover cinnamon rolls as the base makes them taste like a filled Danish to me. They are so easy—just press, fill, and bake! A tablespoon of pumpkin spice can be substituted for the different spices.

5 large or 10 small leftover baked
   cinnamon rolls
8 oz. cream cheese, softened
2 tbsp. sugar
1 egg
1 tbsp. vanilla
1 1/2 tsp. cinnamon

1 tsp. ground ginger
1/4 tsp. ground cloves
1/4 tsp. allspice
1/4 tsp. nutmeg
Leftover cream cheese icing, for
   topping
Toasted pecans, for topping

Preheat oven to 350 degrees.

Press down the middle of each leftover cold cinnamon roll to form a "bowl." Set aside.

In a mixing bowl, beat cream cheese, sugar, egg, vanilla, and spices together until light and fluffy. Fill the middle of the cinnamon rolls with the cheesecake mixture.

Place on a greased baking sheet. Bake for 15 minutes. Let cool.

Drizzle with leftover cream cheese icing and top with toasted pecans. Store in refrigerator.

TO COOK IS TO CREATE: Not a pumpkin spice fan? Think of other spices, flavors, or extracts that could easily be added to the cheesecake batter. How about adding nuts or chocolate chips to the mixture? If you don't have leftover cream cheese icing, simply whisk milk into powdered sugar until the desired consistency, or use rum or brandy instead of the milk to really elevate the flavor. Not an icing fan? Drizzle with caramel.

Leftover Rolls Almond Petit Fours

As a child, I used to love going to the bakery and helping my mom pick out petit fours. One reason was I usually got one to enjoy immediately, and another was I always liked being able to choose the colors of the dainty dab of icing on top. I don't do much decorating on the top of these petit fours, but I do enjoy them immediately after cutting them into squares. These can be personalized to your taste using coffee, rum, or your favorite cordial, or a combination. Irish whiskey and coffee is the combination I enjoy most often.

1 large or 2 small rolls leftover rolls
$\frac{1}{2}$ cup almonds
1 egg, beaten
1 tbsp. sugar

2 tbsp. coffee, rum, liquor, or cordial
1 tsp. vanilla
Icing or cocoa powder for decorating

Preheat oven to 350 degrees.

Cut or break roll into pieces. Place in a food processor with almonds. Process until fine crumbs.

Place crumbs in a mixing bowl. Add egg, sugar, coffee, and vanilla. Mix well. Let sit for 5 minutes, for crumbs to absorb liquid. Mix again.

Press mixture into a buttered dish. Bake for 15 minutes. Remove.

Let cool. Put in freezer for 1 hour or refrigerator overnight.

Cut into squares. Decorate with icing or cocoa powder.

Makes 1 dozen

Brown-Bag Bites

These bites taste like a combination of churros and beignets. They are always a treat if I have a leftover French roll, but they work great with leftover biscuits, too.

1 leftover French bread roll
1 tbsp. butter
1 tbsp. honey
½ tsp. cinnamon

¼ tsp. sugar
Oil for frying
Powdered sugar

Place roll in freezer for 1 hour.

Cut roll into thin slices.

In a microwave-safe container, microwave butter and honey until melted. Stir in cinnamon and sugar. Brush both sides of roll slices. Place slices in a single layer on a parchment-lined plate. Freeze for 30 minutes.

Heat oil to 350 degrees. Fry slices for 30 seconds or until desired crispness. Drain.

Add slices and powdered sugar to a brown paper bag. Give a quick shake. Let cool briefly before enjoying.

Tiny Tidbit: Have a leftover biscuit? Warm and crumble it over vanilla ice cream, and drizzle with honey.

STICKY ROLLS

A word of caution: I have burned my mouth a few times licking the spoon after scooping the sweet syrupy glaze over the baked rolls. I know better, but each time, I fall victim to the brown sugar and cinnamon aroma.

2 tsp. butter
4 tsp. maple syrup
¼ cup chopped pecans

4 tsp. brown sugar
2 tsp. cinnamon
4 leftover dinner rolls

Heat oven to 400 degrees.

Divide butter evenly among 4 wells of a nonstick muffin tin. Bake for 2 minutes.

Stir together maple syrup, pecans, brown sugar, and cinnamon. Divide mixture evenly among the 4 wells. Place rolls top side down over mixture, pressing down gently.

Bake for 10 minutes. Let cool briefly and carefully remove rolls.

Spoon any remaining mixture in wells over rolls.

Makes 4

Orange Almond Rolls

These rolls are so easy fix, for they require no eggs or milk and are ready in less than 15 minutes. Leftover rolls and one lone orange in my fruit bowl were the inspiration for this dish. This recipe uses a whole orange and was modeled after my Sticky Rolls.

1 orange, seeded
1 tbsp. butter, melted
¼ cup sliced almonds, crushed
½ cup sugar, or less depending on
  taste

4 leftover dinner rolls
1 cup powdered sugar

Preheat oven to 400 degrees.

Juice and zest orange. Set aside separately. Slice orange and place in a food processor. Pulse until pureed.

Using a pastry brush, brush butter into 4 wells of a muffin tin. Add 1 tbsp. almonds into each well.

In a bowl, combine orange puree, sugar, and half of orange zest. Slowly stir in enough orange juice to make a slurry. Reserve remaining juice.

Completely coat all sides of rolls in orange mixture. Place rolls top side down over almonds, pressing down gently.

Bake for 8-10 minutes until browned.

In a bowl, add powdered sugar. Slowly stir in remaining orange juice until the desired consistency is reached for the orange glaze. Gently remove each roll. Drizzle with glaze and top with remaining zest.

Refrigerate any leftovers. Gently warm to enjoy again.

Makes 4

TO COOK IS TO CREATE: No rolls? Use stale bread. Simply cut into sticks, dip, roll in almonds, and bake on a parchment-lined sheet until lightly browned. No almonds? Use pecans or walnuts. If you want to up the flavor, add some spices to the orange juice mixture. Try cinnamon, ginger, nutmeg, cloves, or even some vanilla. Want to up the ante on the glaze? Raid the liquor cabinet and use your favorite cordial to make a boozy glaze. I love Frangelico!

Zesty Lemon-Cranberry Rice Fritters

Rice fritters or calas, as they are known around New Orleans, can be made with just about anything and everything. It was one of the reasons why I chose to make them on the Netflix cooking show Best Leftovers Ever! when faced with a fridge of potluck leftovers. If you love beignets, you must give these a try. After all, did you know that beignets are synonymous with fritters? Need I say more? These rice fritters are easy to make, for there is no need to worry about rolling them in flour, egg, and crumbs. The hardest part is craving them and having to wait over an hour before enjoying them.

1 cup leftover rice
4 tbsp. milk
1 tbsp. sugar
1 tsp. salt
Zest of 1 lemon
1 egg, beaten

2 tbsp. dried cranberries
2 tbsp. all-purpose flour
1/2 cup vanilla wafer crumbs
Oil for frying
Powdered sugar for dusting

In a mixing bowl, combine rice, milk, sugar, salt, lemon zest, egg, and dried cranberries. Chill for 1 hour.

Stir in flour and wafer crumbs. Let sit for 5 minutes.

In a cast-iron pot, heat oil over medium heat to 350 degrees.

Scoop 1 tbsp. batter and hold batter close to the oil. Using the back of a spoon, gently roll batter off tablespoon into hot oil. Repeat with remaining batter. Do not crowd the pot. Fry for 2 minutes or until golden brown.

Dust with powdered sugar. Refrigerate any leftovers.

Makes 12

TO COOK IS TO CREATE: During the holidays, I use eggnog instead of milk and gingersnaps instead of vanilla wafers. Think about adding some spices, such as cinnamon, nutmeg, or ginger. Have a flavored sugar? Use it. No lemon? Use an orange. If you don't have dried cranberries, substitute raisins.

Nutty Chip Chip Cookies

These could also be called "bottom of the bag" drop cookies. I always save the crumbs in the bottom of the bag of chips. I either use them as a coating for chicken or make a batch of these cookies. The combination of the sweetness from the chocolate chips and the saltiness from the potato chips makes these cookies the most requested item from my family and friends. For small batches, I prefer to cream the butter and sugar using a wooden spoon the way my MeMaw did, but for larger batches, to save my arm from falling off, I pull out my stand mixer.

1 stick butter, softened
1/4 cup sugar
1/2 tsp. vanilla
1 cup all-purpose flour

1/4 cup crushed leftover potato chips
1 tbsp. chocolate cocoa nibs or chips
1 tbsp. chopped nuts (cashews, pecans, walnuts, or peanuts)

Preheat oven to 350 degrees.

Slice butter into a mixing bowl. Using a wooden spoon, cream butter and sugar. Add vanilla and flour.

Mix in potato chips, chocolate, and nuts. Use a rubber spatula to mix well. Drop by teaspoons onto an ungreased baking sheet.

Bake for 13-15 minutes. Let cool.

Makes 24 cookies

TO COOK IS TO CREATE: What is your favorite potato chip, and how would it change the cookie flavor? Cheese chips and peanuts are a combination I enjoy. What kind of snack could you use instead of potato chips? Pretzels? Yes! Or sub 1/2 cup crushed popcorn. No vanilla extract? Substitute another. Almond is a good one, or even use a liqueur.

Too Quick Cookies

The Swedish meatballs made by my aunt Doris were not the only thing I looked forward to during the holidays. It was also these cookies. One year, as I was steadily snacking on them and chatting with her, she asked if I wanted the recipe. Of course, I did. Here is her recipe in her own words exactly as she wrote it that day. She called them Too Quick Cookies because they cook so quickly. I asked her daughter, my aunt Gennie (older female cousins were always called aunts), if she knew the origin of the recipe. She said it was not long after boxed cake mixes arrived on the scene. She still remembers chopping the candied fruit for her grandmother to make them. Cherries and pecans or candied orange slices and coconut were the two standard cookie combinations. I always passed on the cherry ones but never the chewy orange ones. These cookies are also an easy way to use up bits of nuts left over from holiday baking. Nowadays, many cookie recipes use cake mixes as shortcuts. To me, none are as tasty as my aunt's or bring back as many memories. If she were here, I know she would be delighted to share her cookie recipe with you. She'd tell you to grab a pencil, pull up a chair, and chat for a while. Stay around long enough and you may just hear my uncle Ted's joke du jour. Those were good times.

1 box your favorite cake mix

Add:
$1/2$ cup corn oil
2 eggs also add coconut and candy
   orange slices (cut up)

You can add pecans, walnuts, chocolate chips, raisins, cherries (the kind you use in fruitcake), dates, etc.

Mix well—drop 1 tsp. mixture 2 in. apart on ungreased cookie sheet.

Bake 350 degrees about 8 or 10 mins. Check oven often some cookies bake in less time.

When you bake this type of cookie you can't do anything else it's so fast. If you turn your back your cookies *burn*. Ha!

Tiramisu Cookies

Tiramisu is that delightful blend of coffee-laden ladyfingers, fluffy custard, whipped cream dusted with cocoa powder . . . oh, and, of course, your alcohol of choice. We love tiramisu; in fact, it is one of the desserts Hubby and I actually share when dining out. These cookies give us the taste we love without the overnight wait time for traditional tiramisu and no dinner reservations needed.

1 pkg. ladyfinger cookies
4 tbsp. leftover espresso or strong
   coffee, divided
8 oz. mascarpone cheese, softened
1 tbsp. sugar
1 tsp. liquor (dark rum, Kahlua,
   brandy, etc.)

¾ cup whipped cream
¼ cup almonds, toasted and
   crushed
Cocoa powder for dusting (optional)

Lay the cookies in a single layer in a casserole dish. Brush the cookies with 3 tbsp. leftover coffee.

In a bowl, using a wooden spoon, blend the mascarpone cheese, sugar, liquor, and remaining 1 tbsp. coffee. Fold in the whipped cream. Spoon mixture into a piping bag, and pipe onto each cookie.

Sprinkle cookies with almonds. Dust with cocoa powder, if desired. Store in refrigerator.

TO COOK IS TO CREATE: Can't find any ladyfinger cookies? Use biscotti or shortbread. Think about how easy it would be to change the flavor of these cookies simply by changing the liquor. Don't want any alcohol in your cookies? No problem; simply omit and add your favorite extract, extra coffee, or even flavored coffee creamer! Chocolate lover? Add chocolate chips to the mixture, or top cookies with shaved chocolate.

Cookie Scones

During the holidays, I always make sure to keep a container or two of refrigerated biscuits on hand. With family and friends coming and going, I like to be ready to prepare a simple treat to serve with coffee or tea. A package of 5 biscuits produces 20 scones— that's a good return on investment and yields plenty to share with neighbors, too. These scones can be made with any type of cookie. I like to use a couple of different cookie flavors per batch, keeping the cookie crumbs separate. This is another one of my early non-recipe creations, but don't worry, it's a no-fail, and very versatile one. One of my beloved brunch versions is sugar cookies with champagne added to the orange juice— think mimosa scones! I serve them with fresh berries and a sprinkle of powdered sugar.

1 pkg. 5 buttermilk biscuits $\frac{1}{3}$ cup orange juice, cordial, or liquor
4-5 leftover cookies

Preheat oven according to biscuit package directions.

Crumble cookies into a food processor. Process until they resemble breadcrumbs. Transfer to a bowl. If using different cookies, wipe processor clean and repeat, keeping crumbs separate.

In another bowl, add your choice of liquid.

Cut each biscuit into quarters. Dip all sides of biscuit into liquid and then into cookie crumbs, making sure to coat all sides. Place on a parchment-lined baking sheet.

Bake according to biscuit package directions, checking scones at shortest baking time.

TO COOK IS TO CREATE: Think about the type of cookies you have and what flavors would pair nicely with them. Match the cookie to a flavor. Use what you have on hand for the liquid. Have some eggnog? That's a good choice for gingersnaps, and add a dash of nutmeg, too. Remember you can always add extra flavor to the liquid or crumbs with spices. Have brandy? Use it with pecan shortbread cookies. Irish cream? Try it with chocolate chip cookies. If you're a chocolate lover, melt chocolate, dip a baked scone into it, and let it cool.

Apple Crumble Muffins

These muffins are filled with a simple apple compote and are a great way to use up any overripe or blemished apples. Just two of your favorite apples will be enough to make six muffins. Do not peel the apples, but do save the cores to make the apple-core juice, which adds so much flavor to the glaze for these muffins. The cores are full of fiber and also can be blended directly in your morning smoothie. Apple cider, maple syrup, orange juice, or honey can be used in the compote, but brandy brings a boldness to the apples that I enjoy. I always keep a lookout for places that sell the little airline bottles of liqueurs and liquors. They can be a great addition to the spice cabinet for much less money—no need to buy a big bottle for a couple of recipes. The hardest part of this recipe is letting the apple compote cool. The temptation to stop and spoon some hot apple compote over vanilla ice cream will be strong! If you don't think you can resist, go ahead and double the batch. It will keep up to one week in the fridge. It's tasty heated and spooned over pancakes, waffles, French toast, or oatmeal, too! Be careful getting the muffins out the pan. I don't call them Apple Crumble Muffins for nothing!

2 overripe apples
1 tsp. water
1 tsp. apple cider, maple syrup,
   orange juice, honey, or brandy
$1/4$ tsp. lemon juice
$1/8$ tsp. lemon zest
$1/2$-1 tsp. sugar, to taste
1 tbsp. pumpkin pie or apple pie spice

For the Glaze:
$1/2$ cup powdered sugar
$1/2$ tsp. cinnamon
2 tbsp. apple-core juice*

For the Muffins:
1 cup all-purpose flour
$1/2$ cup sugar
$1/2$ tsp. salt
$3/4$ tsp. baking soda
1 egg, beaten
$1/2$ tsp. vanilla
$1/3$ cup oil
$1/3$ cup chopped nuts (optional)

Roughly chop 2 of your favorite apples. (*Do not peel, and save the apple cores.*)* In a saucepan, over low heat, add the apples, water, and apple cider, maple syrup, orange juice, honey, or brandy.

Add lemon juice, zest, sugar, and spice. Cook, stirring occasionally, for 15-20 minutes. Let cool.

Add compote to 6 wells of a nonstick muffin tin.

Preheat oven to 350 degrees.

To make the muffins, in a mixing bowl, combine flour, sugar, salt, and baking soda. Sprinkle mixture over apple compote.

Blend together egg, vanilla, oil, and nuts, if using. Pour the egg mixture into each well and use a fork to gently blend into flour mixture (without disturbing the compote on the bottom).

Bake for 20-25 minutes or until golden brown and centers bounce back when pressed.

To make the glaze, mix powdered sugar and cinnamon together. Slowly whisk in apple-core juice.

Makes 6 muffins

*Add apple cores to a saucepan. Cover with water. Bring to a boil. Simmer for 30 minutes. Strain juice.

TO COOK IS TO CREATE: What is your favorite spice in an autumn spice mix? Add more to enhance the flavor of the compote. No baking soda? A good rule of thumb is for each $\frac{1}{2}$ tsp. baking soda, substitute $1\frac{1}{2}$ tsp. baking powder. Another extract can easily be swapped in for vanilla—banana is a nice one. For the nuts, I have even used toffee peanuts for a sweeter muffin. Don't like nuts? Use raisins. Want to jazz up the glaze for the kids? Substitute maple syrup for half or all of the apple-core juice. To jazz it up for yourself, use Irish cream!

Sweet Potato Casserole Doughnut Holes

This recipe is a good one not only to use leftover sweet potato casserole or mashed sweet potatoes but also to keep the kids busy, at least for a little while. Let them scoop the mixture and roll it into balls. A mini marshmallow can even be stuffed inside each one for a surprise treat.

1 cup leftover sweet potato casserole or mashed sweet potatoes
$\frac{1}{4}$ cup self-rising flour
$\frac{1}{2}$ cup all-purpose flour

Oil for frying
1 tbsp. sugar
1 tsp. cinnamon
Maple syrup (optional)

In a mixing bowl, blend leftover casserole or potatoes with self-rising flour. Scoop mixture with a melon baller and, using moistened hands, roll into balls.

In another bowl, add all-purpose flour. Roll balls in flour. Set on a parchment-lined plate. Chill overnight or at least 6 hours.

In a deep fryer or heavy-bottomed pot, heat oil to 350 degrees.

Using a slotted spoon, lower balls into the fryer. Fry for $1\frac{1}{2}$-2 minutes until golden brown. Remove with slotted spoon. Drain.

In a mixing bowl, add sugar and cinnamon and mix well. Roll balls in the sugar mix. Enjoy with maple syrup, if desired.

Makes 12 doughnut holes

Tiny Tidbit: When draining canned sweet potatoes, save the liquid. In a small saucepan, over low heat, reduce liquid to make a rich syrup. This makes a perfect dip for these doughnut holes.

Praline Toast

The smell of cooking pralines, the brown sugar patty-shaped candies full of pecans, reminds me of delightful days spent gathering these nuts with my Pawsie. We would walk in the yard, pick up pecans, and put them in an empty ice-cream bucket. He taught me how to distinguish between the good ones and the rotten ones. We would walk and talk all while keeping our eyes down looking for the treasures. We would occasionally eat a couple of pecans but knew the more we saved, the more treats we would have later. We were fortunate to be able to gather pecans by the buckets. This always made my MeMaw very happy. She loved to have bowls full of pecans spread throughout the house, ensuring that any unexpected guests could have a nibble. Looking back, I guess this was her way of tempting her guests with what was to come . . . her famous fudge and pralines! That meant lots of shelling of pecans. But it was fun sitting around the kitchen table "working" with my MeMaw and Pawsie, and then I would go home with a bucket for my mom. Pralines were her holiday treat, too, so I won in both households! This recipe is a good excuse to eat candy for breakfast and a delicious way to share the last praline. I like to use a hearty multigrain bread, but any bread will work. No need to worry if it is stale—the rich praline butter will give it new life. The crunch of the first bite of this toast is one you will never forget, especially if you don't let it cool a minute!

1 leftover regular praline (2 oz.)
2 tbsp. unsalted butter, softened
2 slices bread

Cinnamon (optional)
Chopped pecans (optional)

Preheat oven to 350 degrees.

Crumble praline into food a processor. Process into crumbs.

Transfer praline crumbs to a bowl, and add softened butter. Using a wooden spoon, mix until well blended, then whip the butter for 1 minute until fluffy.

Place slices of bread on a parchment-lined baking sheet. Bake for 5 minutes. Remove from oven. Flip bread slices.

Spread praline butter mixture onto top sides of bread. Return to oven. Bake an additional 5 minutes.

Sprinkle with cinnamon and pecans, if desired.

Tiny Tidbit: Use this whipped praline butter to top baked sweet potatoes.

LAGNIAPPE

A LITTLE SOMETHING EXTRA

Lagniappe means a little something extra or, in this case, a little something extra special to me. The recipes in this chapter are near and dear to my heart. Some are family recipes that I learned directly from my MeMaw standing on my stepstool in her kitchen. Others remind me of special times shared with family. These recipes call up childhood memories, and the tastes transport me back in time.

OLD-FASHIONED SODA SORBET

Just the words "old-fashioned soda" bring back childhood memories of visiting the corner-drugstore soda fountain with my MeMaw and Pawsie. I remember climbing up on the swivel stool, often with a little help from my Pawsie, and feeling so tall sitting at the counter. The day I ran and jumped on the stool by myself was a thrilling day, and so was the day my feet first touched the floor. Both days were cause for celebration—extra scoops were ordered. Root-beer floats for all were the standard. My brother and I never went to the soda fountain together with my grandparents. They took each of us by ourselves for special alone time, but that didn't mean that the other one was left out. The one who went to the drugstore had to pick out a trinket to bring back to their sibling. Tastes evoke strong memories, and I cherish a delicious flashback with two scoops of this sorbet.

12 leftover large marshmallows
1 cup root beer or favorite soda

1 tbsp. lemon juice
Dash of salt

Place marshmallows in a saucepan. Spoon 1 tbsp. soda over marshmallows and heat slowly over low heat. Using a rubber spatula, fold marshmallows over until almost melted.

Remove from heat. Continue folding until smooth and fluffy. Let cool for 1 minute.

Add remaining soda, lemon juice, and salt. Blend thoroughly.

Pour mixture into a shallow tray. Cover and freeze overnight, stirring twice the first hour.

Scoop and serve.

Muffuletta Toasts

I am proud to be from New Orleans, home of the muffuletta. One of my favorite weekend outings growing up was a trip with my dad to grab a muffuletta and a container of black olives. I could smell the aromas from the meats, cheeses, and spices before we walked through the door. It was a treat to get a muffuletta and to scoop the olives out of the large barrels. My dad and I never made it home with any olives. It was our secret tradition. We enjoyed them all by ourselves and often wished we had bought more. A muffuletta, round Sicilian sesame bread filled with layers of olive salad, mortadella, salami, ham, and mozzarella and provolone cheeses, can be served hot or cold. For me to truly enjoy the mixture of flavors, my muffuletta must be toasted. That's how I came up with this idea. One loaf of bread makes two large trays of tasty toasts for a party.

1 loaf white sandwich bread
$\frac{1}{4}$ cup sesame seeds, toasted
$\frac{1}{2}$ lb. sliced ham
$\frac{1}{2}$ lb. sliced salami
6 oz. shredded Italian cheese
   (Parmesan or mozzarella)

$\frac{1}{4}$ tsp. onion powder
$\frac{1}{4}$ tsp. garlic powder
8 oz. olive salad, divided
4 oz. leftover whipped cream cheese
Sliced green olives (optional)

Place 1 slice bread on a cutting board. Using a rolling pin, roll out to $\frac{1}{4}$-in. thickness. Using a 2-in. round cutter, cut out 4 bread rounds. Repeat with remaining bread.*

Place the rounds into wells of mini muffin tins. Sprinkle each with sesame seeds and gently press down, forming a shell.

Preheat oven to 350 degrees.

Place ham and salami in a food processor, and pulse until chopped. Add Italian cheese, onion and garlic powder, and half the olive salad. Pulse a few times, then add remaining olive salad. Pulse until fully incorporated. Transfer to a mixing bowl.

Fold in cream cheese until well combined. Press 1 tsp. muffuletta mixture into each shell. (A piping bag can also be used.)

Bake for 10 minutes. Remove from tins. Top each with 1 olive slice, if desired.

*Here's an idea for all the leftover scraps of bread. Keep the oven on at 350 degrees, and make *croutons!* Simply put them in a bowl, drizzle with olive oil, toss with Italian seasoning, place on a baking pan, and bake for 8-10 minutes or until crispy. They cook quickly, so after 5 minutes, check the pan and give it a shake. These can be frozen, too.

TO COOK IS TO CREATE: What kind of sandwich is your favorite? Make toasts using those ingredients. For example, Reuben toasts would include cream cheese, Thousand Island or Russian dressing, sauerkraut, and Swiss cheese, all pressed into rye-bread shells! Having a kid's party? Bake the shells, then fill with peanut butter and jelly! Have a favorite dip? Try it out in these shells.

Notes:

_____

_____

_____

_____

_____

_____

_____

Pudding in the Clouds

My MeMaw made this treat especially for me. I had it for every birthday and other special occasions and sometimes as a tasty after-school surprise snack: hot chocolate pudding poured over crumbled pound cake to be eaten with a spoon right out of the bowl, my bowl. If I were lucky enough to be present when she poured the pudding over the pound cake, I could enjoy licking the spoon and then digging it straight into the warm pudding. As a child, I called it "Pudding in the Clouds," because the spongy pockets of pound cake reminded me of fluffy clouds. I love the "film" that forms on top of the pudding as it cools. MeMaw would either bake a pound cake or use the few stale slices remaining in the cake box. The slight dryness from a stale pound cake adds a texture dimension to the creamy pudding that makes me always go back for more and more. I will not say how many times I have eaten the whole bowl at one time, but whenever I want to dive back into MeMaw's kitchen, I dive into a bowl of Pudding in the Clouds while it is still warm.

$1/4$ cup grated semisweet chocolate
2 cups whole milk, divided
$1/2$ cup sugar
1 tbsp. 100 percent cocoa powder
3 tbsp. cornstarch

$1/4$ tsp. salt
$1/2$ tsp. vanilla
$1 1/2$ tsp. butter
Leftover pound cake slices

Using a double boiler with water in bottom, or a saucepan with water and a shallow mixing bowl set over it, add grated chocolate and $1/2$ cup milk to the top of double boiler or to bowl. Turn stove to medium heat. Using a wooden spoon, stir constantly to melt chocolate.

When "chocolate" milk is achieved, slowly stir in remaining milk. Stir for 2 minutes. Remove from double boiler and pour mixture into a saucepan. Return to medium heat.

Sift sugar, cocoa powder, cornstarch, and salt together. Gradually add to chocolate milk mixture. Stirring constantly, cook until thickened, about 2 minutes.

Remove from heat. Stir in vanilla and butter until fully combined.

Crumble pound cake into a medium serving bowl. Pour warm chocolate pudding over pound cake. Let sit for 30 minutes, then chill overnight (if you can wait that long!). Grab a spoon and enjoy.

MeMaw always left a little lagniappe in the bowl. Occasionally, I had to share it with my brother.

Notes:

_____

_____

_____

_____

_____

_____

MeMaw's Maque Choux

The one thing I knew for sure before I started this cookbook was that this recipe would be the last one in it. I would not be cooking leftovers if it were not for my MeMaw instilling in me the value of food. Maque choux, pronounced "mock shoe," is simply smothered corn, but there is nothing simple about all the flavors. Her maque choux was the highlight of her summer garden, utilizing the fresh tomatoes and corn that we gathered. I was always delighted to see our pickings come alive in the cast-iron skillet and blossom into a savory meal. My favorite place in MeMaw's kitchen was on my stepstool with the green padded seat. From that perch in the summertime, I learned so much about maque choux and the seemingly endless possibilities it offers. It is also where I learned not to let any of the corn that we harvested go to waste. The smell of the corncob stock simmering and the dish's delightful "popped" corn aroma wafting through the house were and remain teasers of good things to come. For me, there is only one way to serve up MeMaw's Maque Choux, which is just like she did, over a piece of crumbled buttermilk cornbread with an extra slice on the side for mopping up the bowl. On the rare occasion there are any leftovers, I love it cold, stuffed in an avocado, with a little drizzle of oil and vinegar from MeMaw's crystal cruets. There are probably as many maque choux recipes as there are gumbo recipes—family recipes passed down from generation to generation. Like a gumbo, there's a standard base, but then the skillet opens itself to countless variations. Maque choux is an incredible Makeover My Leftover contender, because just about anything can be added. So, fetch the iron skillet.

6 ears corn
2 medium tomatoes, chopped
1/2 tsp. sugar
6 cups water
2 bay leaves
4 slices bacon, roughly chopped

1 yellow onion, chopped
1 bell pepper, chopped
1 clove garlic, minced
1 jalapeno, seeded and minced
1/2 tsp. Creole seasoning
Buttermilk cornbread, for serving

Shuck the corn and set aside husks and silk. In a large bowl, cut the kernels from the cobs, and using the blade of a knife, scrape each cob to remove milk. Set aside cobs.

Stir tomatoes and sugar into the corn. Let sit until ready to use.

To make the corncob stock, add the water and cobs to a stockpot, and bring to a boil over high heat.* Add the bay leaves. Reduce heat to medium low. Cover loosely with lid. Simmer for 1 hour. Add water, 1/2 cup at a time, if needed. Remove from heat. Strain and reserve 1/4 cup stock. Use remainder of stock within 1 week, or freeze to use in soups or sauces.

In a cast-iron skillet, over medium-high heat, cook bacon for 5 minutes. Reserve 1 tbsp. bacon fat in the skillet, and drain remaining into a heat-resistant container (which can be kept in the refrigerator for up to 3 months).

Add onion, bell pepper, garlic, jalapeno, and the ¼ cup corncob stock. Reduce heat to medium low, and cook for 20 minutes, stirring occasionally.

Stir in corn, tomatoes, and Creole seasoning. Reduce heat to low. Cook an additional 15 minutes.

Serve over cornbread.

*Here are some tips to reduce fresh corn waste. After making the cob stock, oven dry the cobs. Place on a baking sheet in a 175-degree oven. Bake for 6-8 hours, flipping halfway through. Let cool. Use dried cobs to fuel campfires or as woodchips when grilling. To feed wildlife, spread dried cobs with peanut butter and sprinkle with birdseed.

Husks can be oven dried the same way (reduce baking time to 2-3 hours). Use for tamales, for kindling, or for crafts.

Husks and silk can also be used to make a stock the same way as the cobs. The woodsy-flavored stock is perfect for tortilla or mushroom soups.

Like to cook with banana leaves? Do the same with corn husks. Quickly rinse husks or soak in beer, wine, or pickle or jalapeno juice. Blot off excess liquid. Use husks to wrap food before cooking—sausage, chicken, fish, or even hot dogs.

Put on your "To Cook Is to Create" thinking cap, start cooking, and have fun.

Index

Louisiana native Susanne Duplantis is an award-winning chef, restaurant veteran, and creator of the food-waste blog, Makeover My Leftover. A certified health education specialist, she has participated in national and international cooking competitions and was a successful competitor at the World Food Championships.

Duplantis works as a recipe developer for national brands, but her passion is eliminating food waste. She conducts food-waste workshops and cooking demos across the state of Louisiana and was featured in the Netflix series *Best Leftovers Ever!* She was a guest on *Tamron Hall* and hosted a monthly cooking segment on Baton Rouge's CBS affiliate, WAFB.

She lives in Baton Rouge with her husband, Chris, and her donkey, Fred.

Illustrator Tom Quaid, a retired cardiologist, has always had a passion for drawing cartoons and caricatures. Upon his retirement in 2009, he opened an art studio, Heart to Art, where he pursues portrait and landscape oil paintings.

Tom and his wife, Susie, live in Baton Rouge, where life is good with six grandchildren.